Cover monotype by Mary-Margaret Moore
In remembrance of her mother.

This book is lovingly dedicated to

**Dr. John Wallace Aiken and
Dr. Louisa Van Sant Aiken**

In deep appreciation and admiration for their life-long service
to humankind and, specifically, for the twelve years of selfless
work and constant support they have rendered to these
teachings. There are no words sufficient to express
the depth of our gratitude.

Let us postulate that you have gone on a journey around the world. Upon completing it, you return home and wish to share your experiences with your loved ones. When you do, you are not going to relate the color of every pebble you stepped on, the view of every leaf on every tree, or the many mundane moments of your trip. What you are going to share are those things that so moved you that you yearn to give them as a personal gift. Some experiences may be difficult, some may be magical, but they all will be memorable.

So it is when you end your life here in the physical body. There will be a pattern of energy to welcome you, and it is likely to say, "What, out of your life, do you wish to show us?" That sharing is the gift of the journeyer who comes home to the beloveds. Out of all you have done, those things you have most loved will come forward for you to give.

Remember please, there is no boardroom of directors to sit you down and ask for an accounting. For most of you, there will only be one, because one great Being of Light is about all a newly freed soul can handle. And it will invite you to tell of your journey. From the very beginning of your life until the very end, the jewels, the gifts will be those times you have loved. Not loved perfectly, just loved the best you could. Please understand this deeply. You are not being judged, you are being guided.

You are being urged to love yourself and your earth plane experience. There is no other statement as important when you die as, "Share with me." And in sharing the moments of your love, there will come an awareness of the beauty and worthwhileness of the whole journey. All the obstacles and events that did not go right, all the things you wish had been different, will fade. And you will understand that by those loving actions in your life, you have added to the love of the Whole.

No one who dies comes up empty-handed of some loving action. No Love ever dies. You carry it in your Being, and give it as a gift. And so is it received, in gratitude. **Bartholomew**

Other books by Bartholomew:

"I Come As A Brother" *A Remembrance of Illusions*
From the Heart of a Gentle Brother
Planetary Brother

Informal tapes and transcripts of talks by
Bartholomew are available from:

Tapes and Transcripts
P.O. Box 98
Taos, NM 87571

Bartholomew books may be ordered directly
from High Mesa Press.

BARTHOLOMEW

REFLECTIONS OF AN ELDER BROTHER

AWAKENING FROM THE DREAM

HIGH MESA
PRESS

1989

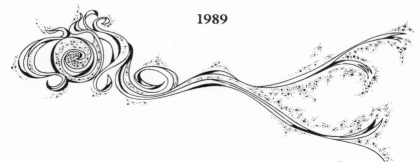

Editors
Joy Franklin
Mary-Margaret Moore

Layout and Design
Joy Franklin

Photography
Carolyn Lake

Word Processing
Phyllis Johnson

Production
Gi

Typesetting
WDType

First Printing October, 1989
Third Printing May, 1990
Fifth Printing April, 1993

THE HIGH MESA FOUNDATION
Post Office Box 2267 / Taos, New Mexico / 87571

M ore than ever before, there is a hunger now for greater spiritual understanding. The Divine is not dead but the awareness of our connection to It is dim. At the dawn of the last decade of the 20th century there is planetary and personal confusion. A feeling of expectancy is present, but we aren't sure if it signals chaos or illumination. Gurus haven't the answer and religion hasn't changed to fill the needs of the individual.

Help is here now. A gentle, more compassionate wisdom is available for those of us who yearn to reawaken the experience of ourselves as a part of God. New teachers come as brothers and sisters to tell us *we* are the Way and the Light. One such elder brother is familiar to us as Bartholomew. Quietly, for over eleven years, this entity has shared 'His' love, wisdom, humor and the conviction we only need awaken to who we are to experience that which we seek. Over and over again, with profound patience, Bartholomew says the same things in different ways, in an unceasing effort to remind us we are *already* enlightened and our lives merely a remembrance of illusions.

In this past year, the power behind 'His' message has grown in intensity and a sense of urgency is present. Whether seated in a workshop, a private reading, another country or listening at a public sharing, Bartholomew's teachings are best transmitted by the spoken word. Our dilemma has been how to translate an oral teaching into written form. More and more, Bartholomew's energy acts as a bridge of understanding between 'His' statements. Gaps between thoughts arise which are unnoticeable when we are together and refuse to translate coherently when we try to pin them to paper.

We have spent many hours rearranging, rewriting and polishing the material we have chosen. Mary-Margaret has been invaluable in this process. Her willingness to call on the Bartholomew energy for additional information has brought a clarity to the work which would otherwise be missed. And as always, the special gift received from being this close to the Bartholomew energy is a deeper understanding of our own processes.

It is with deep gratitude that we present these reflections.

Editor and Staff

CONTENTS

You are more complicated than
you realize and more simple
than you believe.

INTRODUCTION

I n this day and age when every other person you know is doing what is now called 'channelling,' there seems to be a necessity to describe what exactly it is that I do, and why I bother to do it.

First of all, it is important to state that there is nothing that feels 'channelled' about this experience. 'Channelled' as a word seems to reflect a narrowing rather than an expanding...and the one word that seems to best describe what this process feels like is expansion. 'Channelling' sounds as though something from the 'outside' of you is somehow dropped into your body, remaining there until you have said and done what was to be said or done. So what really does it feel like?

The best way to describe the unfolding which takes place is that, as I settle down, a vast silence begins to build within what I call my awareness. I become aware of a feeling-tone that is at the same time still, yet dynamic and extending...silent, yet alive and full of potential. It is very hard to put it into words. When the faces and surroundings have blended into what seems like a soft light, words come. These words come not from some energy that has dropped into my body, but rather from a place within me that is vaster than I usually experience myself to be, that is not confined to 'within me,' but rather removes the barriers of 'inside' and 'outside' until there is only a feeling of One. Not one *thing*, but just One. It is this feeling of present potential that we have named Bartholomew.

Why name this process something like Bartholomew? Why not just 'It'? The name Bartholomew was created by two humans, John Aiken and myself, in 1977[1]. We decided that we needed to call all of this *something,* and when we asked what 'All of This' wanted to be called, the answer was, "Anything you want, but remember—the formless has no name, being beyond the realm of name and form." We decided on Bartholomew as a reminder of that 'persona' in the past life whose name was Bartholomew, that now seems to be 'Mary-Margaret' in this life. All of these distinctions now seem unnecessary, but then was then, and now is now. So 'Bartholomew' as a name came into being as a reminder of that beginning time.

So then, what is Bartholomew? Who knows? It is no *thing,* no *form,* no *person,* no *persona.* It is what it is—wisdom and love and peace. It makes us feel beautiful and loveable and hopeful in its presence. It shines a light on that within us that is most aligned with the God-Self, the beauty and wisdom of our Being. It is a part of the One, and knows itself to be one with the All.

What is all of this for? It seems to me that it has come to help us awaken from the unreal into the real. Perhaps Bartholomew says it best in the following quote:

"The solution to the dream is to awaken. Just keep going by the sweetness of your awareness down to that place in your physical body where there is no dreaming, but rather a seeing of light, a feeling of silence and presence of love. Go there over and over. What happens, my friends, is that this part that has never slept and has no form begins to move closer and closer, enveloping the ego-separated dream. The resulting blend produces no loss, only awakening.

"Understand, you have all dreamt a different dream, and together you have dreamt one dream. If you want help within the dream, I am not the best guide because my job is to help you awaken past that dream world. To talk about the dream characters—how to heal a

dream character or how to bring one back who has left your dream—is not my purpose. You see, I would say that one dream is like another is like another. And there are those who can provide dream-help within the dream-state. But if your desire is to remember that part of you that has never slept or dreamt, then we are in rapport, and I may be able to assist."

Year after year, I see those of us who have listened to the guidance and *practiced* it beginning this awakening. I see us turning away from the belief that the illusion will make us happy, and turning to the only place where real safety lies—within. I see the struggle we have as new temptations arise to turn us back to the illusion for happiness—a new house? A new love affair? More money? But I now sense that we have begun to really learn that, while all these new wonders are delightful and can be fully enjoyed, they are only passing clouds, here one moment, dissolving the next. We seem to be learning that the awareness of the vast sky is the goal, not the passing clouds. We seem to be awakening from the *dream* of who we *thought* we were to the knowing of what is Real.

So I dedicate this book to all of us who have heard what our 'brother' has said, and have kept our vision on the goal-less goal, and have supported one another as we journeyed on this journey that goes nowhere, but is everything. Without each others' support, humor and love, no awakening would have been possible.

Mary-Margaret Moore

---

[1] All of this began when John hypnotized me for a back problem, and sent me into a 'past life,' where we ran into this experience. For further information on the beginning of this process, see the introduction of *"I Come As A Brother," A Remembrance of Illusions.*

AWAKENING FROM THE DREAM

May 21, 1989
Albuquerque, New Mexico

Recently, Mary-Margaret read an interesting article about a bird called the cuckoo. This bird has a capability that may have something to do with your life. When it decides to lay its eggs, the cuckoo looks around its environment and carefully selects the nest of another bird not of its species. Then it copies the color, pattern and size of the host's egg, and lays its own eggs in the host's nest. The eggs are amazingly similar.

Obviously the cuckoo doesn't have an egg dyeing kit, so something else is going on, and that 'something else' has a tremendous amount to say about creative consciousness. We are talking about the consciousness of a bird that is able to decide *ahead of time* what it wants the appearance and size of its egg to be, and then has the ability to create what it desires. It does this so well the host bird accepts the egg as its own.

This behavior is interesting because it illustrates a truth I have been telling you for years—you have the capacity to create on the physical, material plane much more than you believe you can. If this wondrous cuckoo can decide to create eggs of various sizes and colors, do you not think you might be able to create something bigger than an egg for yourself? I grant you, the motivation of the cuckoo doesn't seem to be very exalted. Its desire is to have its egg hatch first so the infant can feed on the other eggs before they come to term. But that too only goes to prove what I have also tried to remind you of, the creative process in itself does not guarantee anything wondrous.

So, why do I bring this forward? I am asking you to partici- pate in the excitement of the idea that this small entity can make a decision and spend the rest of its time making the decision a reality. The key phrase here is "the rest of its time," because as you have experienced, my friends, creation on the earth plane rarely happens in an instant. Once you are outside the belief structure of time-space, things can manifest instantly, but we are working on a physical plane of limitations and one of them is your very definite belief in time and space. Therefore, for this bird, operating under this same law, there is a linear movement in having the idea awaken in its awareness, then the single-pointed intensity to bring that desire steadily forward, and finally manifest it in the material future.

Please take this concept to heart in the deepest sense and understand what is going on here. You have within you the capacity to decide, in this moment, what it is you want to manifest at a future time in your life, and to continue to make the connec- tion with that thought form until it manifests. You do it by holding it steadily in your awareness. The difficulty and the delight in the human consciousness is that you are very diversi- fied. This makes it difficult for you to hold to any one thing that you wish to manifest. You jump from desire to desire because there are so many exciting things for the mind to create. The job is to discipline yourself and your mind toward one goal. It seems obvious, therefore, that great care should be given to your selection.

You have not reached enlightenment because you lack con- sistency. You create now this, now that. There is a certain excite- ment in being a separated consciousness creating and projecting yourself out into your world. Because you have done your job so

well, you have a world overflowing with potential possibilities for
creation. *You are not enlightened because you choose not to be aware
you already are.* And you make this choice, not for some dark, evil
reason, but because you create so well on the separated plane your
creations continue to dazzle you. They seem to promise you
sustained happiness—but if you are observing closely, you will
find they do *not*. You will not find sustained happiness and
enlightenment by creating things that rise and fall. Your happiness comes when you decide to stop creating alone, and begin to
create from that area of yourself where the Light is found.

Many of you are trying very hard to come to what you call a
state of love. This means you want to have, as many moments as
you can, an open heart and a state of harmlessness moving
through your awareness, so everything you touch, see or even
think about receives from you only that which is pure, that which
is closest to the God within you. On one level, every one of you
knows what you want because everyone wants the same thing.
Whether consciously or unconsciously, you want to know, with
an assurance beyond all doubt, there has never been such a thing
as sin or guilt, and you reflect a part of God that is pure, loving
and wise. But if you are paying attention, you will see you fail to
achieve this every day. And please, this is not something to cry
about. It is simply the way it is, and until the magical moment
comes when you acknowledge this, you will continue to try to
find something outside yourself to meet the need you have to see
yourself as pure, happy and wise.

To experience your absolute purity, you must know you have
never 'sinned' against anyone else, no one has 'sinned' against
you, and nothing wrong has really ever happened in the deepest
sense. The moment you decide you truly want that experience,
you stop paying attention to the 'outer.' You will come to see no
matter who you are looking at, no matter what is happening,
whether it be loving or life-threatening, the other person is
looking for the same thing you are. They are looking to you and

through you for a reflection of their perfect purity. They are looking for the knowledge they have never done anything wrong.

Who do you want to be? Literally, sit with this question awhile. Part of the reason for sitting is to give you an opportunity to quiet down so you have a chance to identify what you wish to consistently experience in yourself and in your world. Give yourself the opportunity to remember your happiness depends on one thing—you experiencing yourself as a part of God. Once that awareness is yours, you move into those very simple, basic energy fields you have come to identify with God Consciousness; that consistent, never-deviating sense of love, of peace, of brilliant joy, and total awareness. That is what you all seek.

Creation In The Manifest World

Somewhere during the process of creation you made the mistake of believing the body itself has the power to create. From this mistaken belief, you get the idea the cells of your body can run amuck on their own and create all sorts of horrible illnesses. You also have the idea the way to cure these cells exists only on the physical plane. If that is your belief, it is helpful to go to the physical and remedy the situation as best you can on that level. But it is not where the real cure comes from. The body did not create the illness, and the body cannot cure it. So what really happens?

You are afraid that somehow your body will be able to create things you do not want and you believe these creations have nothing to do with your thoughts or your emotions. What a frightening concept, that somehow the physical body, without ever turning around and asking the rest of you, can create something that harms you. The idea that a part of your psyche can run renegade is what frightens you. There is a sense of being out of control. It's very much like being on a wild horse without any reins or means to guide it in any way.

The solution is simple. I did not say it was easy, but it is simple. You must realize it is the mind which has given endless messages to the physical body, and in so doing, the physical body, following those messages, creates certain things. 'Fixing' those things does not occur in the physical. Real healing takes place on the level of the mind, and that is where you must meet your fear, taking your creative powers and directing them into the physical body. The physical body then creates along the lines of the newly-given directives.

Now let's go back to the lesson from our wonderful cuckoo. *The bird observes what it wants to create, and then moment after moment affirms it. By holding the thought, its creation manifests exactly like it.* None of you are stunned at that statement, yet I would like to tell you, whatever your life looks like today is because you have been concentrating on certain thoughts which have brought your life into its present form. You have formed your life with your thoughts. It is not your renegade body that has done the creating, it is your renegade *mind.* You are creating right out of your limited belief system.

When people come to me, I tell them to be responsible for what they create with their thoughts. They say, "No, no. I don't want to have anything to do with what I create. I want God to create for me." Well, I ask, how are you going to do that? "Ah, I'm not going to do anything, and God will create whatever God wants and it's alright with me." But of course, if you are not going to create with consciousness, then your unconscious will do the creating for you and your ego-based unconscious is not God. Lack of attention ends up with unconscious creations. Why does every teacher say stay in the moment? Because in the moment you hold the reins of creation and the renegade unconscious is gently, obediently placed under your control. When you are out of the moment the renegade can run amuck, creating what you no longer want out of reliving the past or fantasizing the future.

My friends, again and again I ask you to take seriously the power of your magnificent, wonderful mind. You are afraid of your mind, of what it has created, because you believe you have created a separated world that is no longer joined with God. You believe the power of the mind is so great you can create a world God is not interested in, where this separation is all there is unto eternity. Despair comes when you see the horrors you have created, and you fear creating more of the same. But God only allows the free play of your awareness to create—*within certain limits*. The Divine within you has placed limits past which you cannot go. You are afraid of being responsible for what your mind creates, so you try not to pay attention to your thoughts. By not paying attention, you go on creating right out of the shadow part of your unconscious. When you really understand this, you can choose to stay in the moment and remember what it is you really wish to create. This gives you the power of conscious choice. Then you create as you *choose* to create.

Let us go back to the assumption that each one of you would like to know yourself to be totally sinless and totally harmless and to see yourself still as that clear, pristine Light of God Awareness. You all deeply remember the wonder of that beginning explosion. You remember the pristine purity, the abundant Light, and the clear consciousness that exploded from God and became you. A part of you has never forgotten, and it is that part which keeps pulling you, keeps saying, "Compare your separated, fearful awareness to me. Compare it to your remembrance of me." So, allow the remembrance because a part of you has never forgotten. Victory is within your grasp. Please sit this day and allow yourself to feel sinless, to feel as if you were nothing but pure light and power, and you have done nothing but radiate the light and wonder of who you are. By allowing this feeling to come up again and again, you give it life, you give it power, you give it reality. Dare to allow yourself the unthinkable, to feel your deepest desire to be the Divine. If you do, the first step, which is the very largest, has been taken. Once you understand and feel what it is you really want, the second step is to acknowledge what *you* want, *everyone* who comes into your life also wants.

Most of you have been fortunate. You have had love, support and some degree of power or prestige. No one would be here who did not experience even a glimpse of that in their lives. But through it all, the height of the most ecstatic awareness, comes the feeling it's not enough. You know at any moment these things can turn on themselves and be gone, or if not gone, lose their meaning. You have had your billions upon billions of moments when that which you have sought has come to you in the full flood of its power, wonder and beauty. If there is anything you long for now you think you do not have, let me tell you, in some lifetime you have already had it. And here you are, still wanting the same things over and over again. The solution is to desire something else, something lasting.

Why all the concern over what you create? Because you are in pain. When you are creating fear, anger, resentment or self-pity, it is of concern because it hurts you. If all of this didn't hurt, would you care? Would anyone care? If somebody came up and shot you and it was a blissful feeling, if your emotional body was violated and you felt nothing but rapture, would you be making such a fuss? You fuss because it hurts. You can be hurt on the physical, emotional and mental levels. That's why you need something to come along and move you out of fear and pain. If there was none, there would be no quarrel with what you have created.

The way out of fear and pain is simple. It is to remember—remember what it is you want to feel, what you want to have running through your mind, your emotions and your body. From that level the choices become very simple. Choose what you can do to let those around you sense *their* innocence, *their* purity and *their* beauty, and those very things will grow in you. Just as the bird holds its awareness on what it wants to make manifest, you hold in your awareness what you wish to make manifest, in you and in your life. Just remember you want the sense you are sinless, that harmlessness has always been in place, and peace is ever-present. Return again and again to that remembrance and you will change your life.

You are asleep. You do not know who you are because you are asleep, but you can awaken. You can awaken today, because in the realm of the Divine there is no such thing as time-space. Things are merely out of focus, and with a slight readjustment of the lens, miraculously, in one moment, it all comes into focus. Everything is seen clearly. You *will* awaken from the dream, either now or later. Why not now?

You must be willing to be a co-creator with God. A co-creator is one who decides what attributes of God-Self they want to experience and then concentrates on those attributes until they appear.

YOUR LIFE IS PERFECT

February 11, 1989
Taos, New Mexico

Caught in the duality of earth plane awareness, it is the human psyche's job to learn how to move between the polarities as they manifest in the world. This is a dualistic planet and its function is to be dualistic and present you with various opportunities to understand the play of these energies. The rhythm of duality is the postulation of opposites: left, right; good, bad; male, female; light, dark; any you may want to present. At its most painful, dualism represents itself as you and other. So when pain arises, a part of your awareness understands you have fallen into ego-based energy, and the function of that energy is to see itself as separate.

It is the job of the ego-based consciousness to keep you moving, to keep you interested, to keep you delighted in the dance of polarity. But on some level, you all know there is nothing dependable in that kind of motion. For example: One morning you arise and are truly filled with the love of God. You look out upon the beauty of the world, you are moved, and you feel Love. As you interface with different parts of your world, your feeling is picked up by those around you and then, someone slams a door in your face. And the difficulty comes when you cannot hold the love. Some event or response from your world puts you back into fear, anger, resentment or self-pity. No matter how hard you wish it to be, your love is not dependable. It does not have the consistent, deep, open, abundant heart-power you want, and well you know it.

There is a tremendous amount of excitement in the play of dualities until you begin to pay attention to the contents of them. Once you do, you will become aware of the repetition. Most of the content is based on future or past, redoing, resaying, or rethinking. The problem with that kind of focus is the lack of *grounding power* as you swing between the poles of duality. Grounding is done in the moment. Grounding gives you a feeling of deep security and safety. Without it, suffering results. Suffering begins and extends from the mind. Hope is possible with awareness because *you* are in control of its focus. Whatever game of duality you might be playing contains a certain amount of ego-based power, but when you decide there is another layer of your Being you can move to which has nothing to do with duality, you will find yourself on the way to becoming consistently loving.

On the other hand, none of you are consistently unloving. When someone says you are not a loving person, they most often mean there are times you are loving and there are times you are not. And they are very conscious of the times you are not and will be sure to inform you of them! There is no one that is not at some time and to some degree loving. But when the world says you are this or that, or you should be this or that, understand their frustration. They have given you the responsibility of showing them 'love,' just as you have given them the responsibility to show you 'love.' In the end you will both be disappointed because no one in the separated awareness can be consistently loving. *To whatever degree you have placed the responsibility for your feelings of love and wholeness on someone else, is the degree to which you are bound to disappointment.* There is only one place where dependable love is found, and it is that place within you where Divine Love and Light await your awareness.

The quality of your state of consciousness is your responsibility. It takes an outer stillness to enable you to become aware of your inner power. When you are interacting with others, you fall into the projections of duality more easily. No blame. This is why I ask if you are really committed to moving through the world's polarities and resting in the Wholeness of the heart. To do this, you must practice stillness over and over. You need to allow all of your Wholeness to reveal itself to you, silently and intensely.

Pain Is Not Necessary To Find God

Does your life contain suffering? You have the idea you are suffering as a punishment. But, one's own mind does the punishing, and the overwhelming combination of like minds on the earth plane creates punishment. When you control your mind, you help control your destiny. *It is not true God created your suffering. You did!* As human consciousness became aware it had splintered itself off from the Source and created a separate, manifest world, it realized the feelings of that world did not reflect Wholeness. It was noted over time, that *pain* served best to remind you looking outside yourself for peace and Wholeness was wrong. Pain became one of the methods you chose to move your attention from the external to the internal world, but it does not have to be *the* way! If you continue to believe, as your ancestors have taught you, that you can only find God through suffering, then you will, by the directive of your own thoughts, continue to suffer and make yourself and others miserable so you can 'go Home.' Suffering is historically very effective, but would you not prefer to discover who you are without the prod of pain? Once you deeply understand what the other choices are, you need not continue to use pain. It *is* a choice, and you choose it thought by thought.

Your mind is always searching, like a squirrel always searching for acorns. The squirrel sits, surrounded by the acorns it has gathered. Is it seated 'blissed out' in the midst of acorn consciousness? No! The squirrel is wondering where it can find its next bunch of acorns. With all due respect, this is also what your ego-based mind has in store for you. Its basic rule is to never completely satisfy you, to keep you looking for the next treasure, constantly searching for the fulfillment of your next desire. It is important you understand the force of your desires. They are addictions and being addicted to anything simply means you feel there is something you need to make you Whole *that you do not have*. And you are all looking for Wholeness in the wrong place. You do not *know* how to find it. You 'think' you know. You hope you know. And you try to get people around you to tell you that you do know. But you don't, and that's part of the dilemma. So, where do you go to find this Wholeness? If you choose to use the power of each moment as it presents itself, to pull you in and rest you in the center where Being is experienced, you will find your

Wholeness. You will find who you really are. You will experience pure, conscious awareness.

My friends, if it were at all possible, do you not think those who have reached the summit of awareness would not turn back and bestow it on everyone remaining on this creative planet? Of course they would. But it cannot be done. All we can do is remind you of the way out. The way out is down, through the judgment and separation. The goal is to rest deeply in that inner place of safety where you can find the love and compassion that connects you to the One God. Your concern with fear and judgment keeps you on a circular treadmill, moving endlessly around, when the way off is so simple. Remove your attention from fear and judgment, drop down to that space of safety, and do it a hundred times a day, a thousand times a day, or however many times it takes, until one day that's all that is present.

Your life is exactly the way it is for one basic reason: the vastness of your Being knows the perfect scenario to help you decide how to deepen your connection with the Light. Your Wholeness has as its single goal your awakening to your God-

Self. You *are* pure, conscious awareness. Any other definition of you is false. Start paying attention and you will find that which separates you from the Light is your judgment against yourself, other humans, and the world. Your *judgments* keep you from knowing, feeling, experiencing, and exploding into Light, and that is the *only* thing that separates you. You are not seeing what is real. At any moment, there is the beautiful potential possibility of bursting into full conscious knowledge of who you are.

You *can* remember what you are looking at is not as it seems. You *can* remember it is a lie created by the separated senses and you don't have to believe it. You do not have to become good, pure and holy to experience Wholeness. There is no such thing as goodness, because goodness denotes the necessity for evil. Those are words of judgment. Either you have the awareness of *pure consciousness* or you have the awareness of *ego-based confusion*. There are no other choices, my friends. There *are* no other choices.

Decide that you are in control of your awareness. Your consciousness is placed somewhere *by you* each moment, so every moment you have a choice to make. You either remember you are seeing camouflage and move behind it or you become trapped by your dualistic vision. You say this is hard to do—but compared to what? Start paying attention to your thoughts and you will realize they cause much more difficulty, are much more debilitating, and much more aligned with energy loss, than the focused awareness of dropping to a place of stillness within you. When you begin to go deeply within, literally hundreds of times a day, that wonderful sphere of pure consciousness, which is you, becomes the focus of your energy. You feed *something* every time you think, so *you* must decide what it will be. Do you want to feed your separation, your alienation? It *will* increase. Do you want to feed your Wholeness? It, too, will increase. You are the way to Truth and Light. *You* are the way! Gather up your awareness and place it where *you* wish it to be and it will stay there, fixed, until you move it again. It's really up to you.

Who Is God?

It might be helpful now to take a moment to talk about this God you say you're looking for. Let's examine your beliefs about 'Him'. The logic usually goes like this. The child is like the father, therefore the father must be like the child. Really? Do you really believe that God, 'the Father,' is just a stronger, more powerful, more overwhelming replica of you, of all the humans on this earth plane? Many of you *do* believe this consciously or unconsciously, and this belief is what catches you. You believe that you, in your ego-based consciousness, and God are the same. And then you ask why you are afraid to experience God. Why would you not be afraid? Do you really think human consciousness blown up a million times would represent a loving God? Humans punish and treat each other with cruelty, so with your logic, God, who is like you, will also treat you with the same cruelty and punishment. But it is *all in your mind.*

The way out is not to add another lie to this illusion. The way out is to experience the unthinkable, the unspeakable. When you claim, moment after moment, that your life is perfectly in order, and you picked it for your own particular illumination, that truth begins to filter down and change you. In acknowledging everything is perfect, the Beingness of you says, "If everything's perfect, then everything is in perfect alignment for me to see the Light." You can reprogram the parts of you which really believe this is not true, that something has to change and be different for you to experience the Divine.

If the moment is perfect, then the moment is *now.* If you don't believe it is possible now, then it won't be now. How do you make yourself believe something you don't believe? By choosing to place your awareness on those things that are Light filled, for as long as it takes you to know the Truth. The greatest obstacle to knowing your full enlightenment is the belief you are not now enlightened. What you have been saying is, "God, stay away, I'm not good enough. I'm not pure enough," and finally, "Don't come because I'm terrified of what You might be if You did come."

There *is* Light. It is filled with the most amazing, abundant love, power, and delight you could possibly imagine, and if you keep looking for it every moment, you *will* start to feel it without anything outside of you changing. God has no favorites, so He is not going to pick your illumination over that of another. When God is present, miracles always happen and resolution of all differences is possible. Everyone benefits. When you decide you need to be separate to find God, people in your life get hurt. "Seek ye first the Kingdom and all else will be added unto you." With your separated consciousness, you don't know what's best for you and others. Those of you who are worried about all of your obligations, don't worry. You have no idea how well God can take care of your obligations. That's not your job. Your job is to seek the Kingdom, or Light, as it's unfolding, *doing whatever is in front of you with the highest awareness you are capable of.*

On the deepest level, there is nothing wrong with what is going on now. Your life is perfect and you picked it. Once you experience the truth of that statement day after day, you *will* know who you are. Your life is perfect and *you* picked it. Don't believe those fairy tales that tell you if you get everything right, you will live happily ever after. You can never get everything right so you will never live happily ever after in the world of separated vision. The Wholeness of you has gone through an incredible amount of trouble to get you to just where you are, hoping you will pay attention to what is happening in the moment. The perfect place to be is wherever you are.

There is a power within each of you that will reveal the Truth should you ask for it. Turn to it again and again. Don't worry about thoughts, just drift through them down into the feeling you are looking for. Words and thoughts rise and fall. Focus your awareness and drift through your ego debris down to a point where it's very, very still. Be still and know you are a part of God.

Keep remembering the God attributes you truly want to manifest. When doubt comes in, ask yourself if your life isn't fuller acting as if there were a God for you to blend with. What have you got to lose by continuing to feel the dream?

WHO AM I?

February 19, 1989
Albuquerque, New Mexico

Who are you? Today, I am going to answer this question, and for those of you who can hear and believe me, the journey is almost over. You are *pure, conscious awareness.* That is who or what you are. Anything else is a manifestation of the idea and the belief in separation. Anything else ties you into concepts of endings, beginnings, endings and beginnings. Anything else creates a belief structure that moves you inexorably between the two poles of positive and negative that make up the polarity of this planet.

I have made the statement that you are limitless, and every great Awakened One says again and again there are no limits. *You* have placed *yourself* in limitation. Limitations are of the small mind, created from a separated consciousness, aware of beginning and end. *Anything, my friends, you perceive that has an end or a beginning is not who you are.* It is true you are here manifesting a sense of separation for the moment. But you have been caught and locked into that illusory thought-field of separation. The only thing going on in and around you, throughout this entire planet, throughout *all* of the createdness, is *energy in motion.* That is all!

If you stop a moment and look at your thoughts, you will run right into the mediocrity of your small mind. To keep the game of separation going, you must remain totally unaware of what you are thinking about most of the time. You leave your home and find yourself at Safeway when you really meant to go in the opposite direction. In the midst of talking to people, stop and ask yourself what you have just said. Most of you would not remember.

You are not present in your own mind because you know it holds nothing lasting—it is for the most part, mediocre. Do I dare to say that some great thoughts such as Einstein put forth are mediocre? Well, my friends, no matter what the thought, compared to the feeling of who you really are, it is all mediocre. You are trapped in this mediocrity of constant thought, judging others and judging yourself. On it goes, constant judgment, trying always to make some kind of assessment of where you are in relation to other. So you become agitated because you sense that, if this unending rising and falling of the mediocre substance of mind-stuff is all there is, it may not be worth going on. This knowledge can be a prison of incredible intensity. How can you possibly align this vision with the statement that you are limitless?

I cannot tell you 'the' way out because there are many. If you find one that ignites your heart into the awareness that you want freedom from your limitations more than anything, I urge you to follow it with all your strength. There are as many ways to freedom as there are people, because each heart has its own journey, and each awareness has its own experience. Each of you knows exactly where you are trying to go.

Practicing The Stillness

Deeply, magnificently and wondrously alive within your physical body is the entrance to the source of the God-Self. It is there and you touch upon it through silence. To many of you, silence means meditation. But the fast path to the Source, through deep and intensive meditation, is not available to many of you, so let us talk about what is. The first thing you must drop is the belief there is something you must change in order to

experience inner silence. You have the idea that silence means
stopping every motion of your physical body, and all the energies
around you, thus placing yourself in a vacuum.

Since energy is always in motion all around you, you set
yourselves an impossible task. Your psyche, your wholeness,
knows the way to the silence of your Being. You need not know
how to do it, but you must *want* to. You must give yourself the
quiet directive to be still. It's as if you hold your breath in the
beginning. Close your eyes, hold the breath, feel the stillness
inside yourself, then go about whatever needs to be done.

You are pure, conscious awareness and any other definition
of you is a lie. But if this is so, where is Love? The reason I do not
dwell on the word Love is because it has a mundane feeling to it
when it moves through the human consciousness. You have not
yet realized that your heart and mind are filled with the Light of
Love. And the Light of Love *is* pure, conscious awareness.
Awareness and Love are identical. Love is what awareness feels like! As
you decide to believe there is such a thing as Divine Love and you
are that, you will yearn to silence the endless chatter of your life in
order to reach a place where you know it. You are total Love and
total Compassion, and this creates a feeling of wondrous uplift-
ment that fills the mind, the heart, and the physical body when
you touch upon it.

If you choose to practice this silence, certain things will open
up to you. They will start when you begin to know there *is*
something inside and all you have to do is ask for the silence to
feel it. As you practice the stillness, wait for the response with
expectation. Don't forget the expectant waiting. Oftentimes, you
pray and you pray, and just when God is getting ready to answer,
you get up and leave. The response to your yearning to know the
essence of who you are is available instantaneously, but you've got
to be expecting to feel it. If you want to know who you are, if you
want to experience pure, conscious awareness, limitless, without
judgment, without any kind of duality, begin to give yourself the

directive, "Be Still." The Wholeness of you knows precisely what your deepest yearning is and in the expectant stillness, you will experience Who You Are.

My friends, I have said this before but let's say it again. Your Wholeness, your entire psyche, has one main directive—bring this separated one to the knowledge there is but One Self. *There is but One.* Every event you choose for your life, no matter how destructive, chaotic or miserable it may seem, has been allowed to manifest because your Wholeness has an innate knowledge of those things you need to get you to the place where you will choose to sink deeply within, into the stillness of who you are.

When you awoke to the realization you had separated your-self from the silence of the Divine, and all you could now hear was the chatter of your mind, you felt the deep pain and isolation of that knowledge. A part of you wanted to experience the silence of the One again, no matter the cost. Pain and suffering work for you because, in the times of your pain and suffering, you seek God. If you hear nothing else, please hear this. Suffering comes to remind you to put aside all the chaos of your judgmental ideas of who you are and rest deeply in who you *really* are. Is it not possible, if you consciously decide to live in the silence without pain and suffering, that pain and suffering may not be necessary? You can find God through your own sweet will. You do not need to run away from pain, just *toward* joy and beauty and wonder. It is your choice. Because this is a planet of polarities, *if you can find God through pain, there has to be a way to find God through joy.*

Reflected Consciousness

When you fall into the place of the silent Self, there is no time, there is no space, there is no you and other. That is the 'salvation' of this whole process. If it took as many years to undo the illusion of separation as it did to create it, you would have a long way to go. Inner awareness has no time-space sense to it at all. One experience of that place within and you will never be

fooled again. You will never look out onto 'them' and 'me.' You
will know it's all contained inside you. You are limitless. Pure,
conscious awareness is limitless.

How do you experience that state? Practice and more practice. Conscious awareness has a *focus* to it. Most of the time, the
focus of your consciousness is 'out there.' It's like a powerful
searchlight originating from within you and shining out. It lights
up anything your eye looks upon and illuminates it. When you
take this focus of conscious awareness and reflect it back on itself
through going within and being silent, it will also illuminate
itself. Every moment of your life you are illuminating some part
of consciousness. When it's outside you, it's the separated consciousness. These thoughts are not pure, conscious awareness.

The world is a camouflage, a camouflage that is lying about
the totality of who you are and who everyone and everything else
is. You lie to others and they lie to you. You are constantly
commenting on yourself, on others, on your performance, on
their performance. You are brilliant critics. Pay attention to what
you dwell on and you will realize it is an endless critique. No
blame. Separated ego consciousness experiences life as an ongoing critique. You can stop this endless process by using your inner
and outer world in a maximum way. Use those still inner
moments, and at the same time discipline your awareness to
remind you of the outer camouflage around you and move
beyond it. In the beginning this kind of exercise is contrived. In
the beginning you are constantly deciding whether you really
want to continue your critique of the world or whether it might
be more peaceful to remember it's a camouflage. So you must
re-train yourself. Creating separation took a tremendous amount
of psychic concentration and time. It will not take as much time to
get back to the Source because what you created with your ego
was false. I am not asking you to reform your ego or make it
perfect. You are doing the best your ego can do. But I am asking
you to turn from the critique and begin to remember what you

are and who you are.

Take a few moments to close your eyes and become aware of your thoughts. If you want motivation for moving away from thoughts, nothing works better than the observation of them. After closely observing thoughts without judgment, gently pull your awareness away. You *will* want out of that continuous round of sameness. Pull your mind away and go to that place within where there is perfect balance, where there is nothing but consciousness, nothing but Light, nothing but Love, nothing but total Knowing. It is a lie that you cannot reach it! It is a lie, and such things as sorrow, pain, suffering, loss and illness are not needed to reach it. Tell yourself you've got the picture. You know what you need. You can find your way Home, so you don't need pain to guide you anymore. Then prove it to yourself by gently and firmly pulling yourself back to the silence and to the feeling of the stillness. With all due respect, *you* created the idea that suffering could bring you Home. God created the idea that beauty, wonder, delight and peace could bring you Home.

The way out of sorrow is to be grateful toward whatever pain you created to move you closer to God. For just an instant say, "Thank you." The energy field of pain and suffering you are pushing against is strong and pervasive. Sometimes you just have to grit your teeth and say, "Thank you. Thank you," to push through it. You picked this life because you knew it would contain the experiences necessary to reunite you with God. And it will not fail.

Inspiration does not come from the ego.

HAWAII WORKSHOP

February 25, 26 and 28, 1989
Maui, Hawaii

Why have some of you gone to considerable sacrifice in one way or another to travel all the way to Hawaii to be here today? It is because your Deep Self, the very deepest part of you that you would call the God-Self, had something very specific in mind for you to experience. You are not here just to enjoy the beauty and the sunshine. The reason you have come this far, at this particular time, does not touch the finite mind. The vast part of your Being has been trying to guide you every moment of your life. You thought you were in this by yourself, struggling through your journey alone. But this is not true.

Every movement you have ever made has been made by your small self in the presence of your Deep Self. It is comforting knowledge to realize you have never done anything alone. When you know this to be true, the emotion you call *guilt* will cease to exist. Guilt separates you from God's Love and you can either move through your life with guilt, or make another choice. If you have begun to feel that guilt is something which darkens the soul and kills your joy, and if you are truly ready to release guilt, you can choose again. Let us use this time together to choose again.

No matter how well you are 'behaving' now, you know you have 'misbehaved' in the past, and there is every likelihood you will 'misbehave' in the future. The idea you are able to sin without the comfort and support of the God-self means you think there is something you can do without Divine Presence. But please hear this—*if the Divine were not present in every moment, you would not be present either*. If you both are present, then where is the guilt? *Do you really think God feels guilt?*

Would you like to be enlightened and guilt-free? Some of you would and some of you are not quite certain. Some of you are afraid you would lose your sex appeal or your money or your mind. And some of you would feel guilty about not feeling guilty! But don't worry, wherever you are at the moment is alright. You will eventually realize you have had enough of guilt and will no longer wish to live in a state separate from God. Therefore, eventually, you will do anything necessary in order to bring that knowledge of guiltlessness deeply into your being.

You've read all the books, but it is not reading that brings revelation. Reading brings intellectual learning. Revelation, the understanding of what is really going on, is experiential, and you have to *decide* to experience it. You have been tricked into believing you are only a physical body. But you are not. You are pure, conscious awareness, *manifesting* in a body. Anything else you believe yourself to be is not true—not true in the sense that whatever arises through birth goes through a cycle of living, and then falls into death. This ongoing cycle is not what you really are. You need to touch upon the part of your being that is Eternal, the part that feels the perfection of life in the midst of chaos and guilt.

As you look across the globe and see disaster, pain and loss, a question must arise. With all these difficulties surrounding you, how do you dare to leave it all behind and come to this beautiful island to find God? For many of you, this question will cause immediate guilt. How can you have so much when so many have so little? Do not underestimate guilt. It is constantly present in your life in many ways, asking how you dare be happy when the rest of the world is miserable. Do not think you are free from this

response. Your hearts are open enough to be sensitive to the
suffering of this planet. Unconsciously the guilt arises and points
a finger, saying, "How dare you be immersed in the feeling of
pure, expanded awareness? How dare you taste bliss while this
planet suffers?" Unless you make the decision to stop this spiral,
you will fall deeper and deeper into this kind of guilt as the
planetary difficulties increase.

Take a few moments to answer these questions. They are relevant
wherever you are in your life now. Sit quietly and easily, then move your
awareness to the rising and falling of your breath. Take your time. Now
bring your attention to the heart center and feel the rising and falling
of breath there. Just breathe, gently rising and falling. When you are
securely centered here, gently bring forward the question, "Why me?" or
"How dare I?" then just wait. You are waiting for that wonderful,
uplifting feeling of the heart that comes when you ask to become aware
of the absolute perfection of your life—perfect because each part of it has
brought you to this place, this day. Nothing could have been left out,
nothing changed, nothing erased. Your being is perfect just as it is. And
*this perfection of your being is not a thought, my friends, it's a **feeling**.*
Look inside, expecting to feel the perfection. Please stay with this until
that feeling arises.

Pause until finished.

Do You Want To Be Free?

There comes a time when you decide to change your view of
yourself as an individual ego-based consciousness that is trying to
be happy as a body. You decide to stop feeling guilt and to start
feeling free of limitation. How do you drop the bottom out of
guilt? You do it by moving from your ego-identity to your identity
as a being of Light. The best tool I can give you to drop into your
Light Self and live from there is to remind you of something you
have been told many times—*what you concentrate on you will
experience!* If you ask, you will receive. If your eye is single, your
being will be full of Light. Learn to perfect this skill, and you will

know you are the Light.

Conscious imagination, carefully used, can be part of a creative approach to finding the Light. You are always imagining, but the only real thing happening is what is happening now, you are sitting in this place, on this floor, now. That's it. Any other description of what is going on is imagination. The children, the car, the grocery list, all imagination. There is only one real thing, and this is it. All the rest of your world could be dead. You could have lost all your loved ones and not know it. All you know is what you have in this moment, in this instant in time-space, wherever you may be. Anything else is a mechanism to grab you and keep your ego-based polarities moving back and forth. If you watch your mind, you will see the truth of this—your mind is constantly creating unreal events over and over, and they never become real. This kind of imagining needs to be left behind. You need to move to the Self.

The way to the Self, the way to the 'non-me,' to the universal Wholeness, is simple. First use conscious imagination to *image* what you want, and then put the power of your awareness on those images to make them manifest. Your conscious awareness is always focused on something, whether you are aware of it or not. That is its nature. Most of the time awareness is focused on whatever you are thinking about. Whatever it lights up it makes stronger, connects you to more definitely and brings closer to your reality. Thoughts are the building blocks of what you experience. God is the Building Block of awareness. In two minutes we could create hell on earth in this room just by focusing on all of your secret, private hells. Concentration increases the power of *what* you concentrate upon.

Clear, conscious awareness focuses on whatever is in front of it, and that focusing makes real, stronger and more intimate whatever it lights up. You are not separate from the things you focus on, my friends. I ask you to think about that. You are not separate from *any* thought you focus upon. Your awareness does not say you are focusing on somebody else, on someone else's imperfections. It doesn't know the difference. If your awareness is on another, whatever your thought pattern about them, your awareness experiences it *as you*. It does not differentiate between your thoughts about someone else and thoughts about yourself. It simply focuses on whatever is before it and makes it more real. That is why I ask you to be aware of what you are thinking.

When you turn conscious awareness *on itself*, what happens is *enlightenment*. Pure, conscious awareness, focusing on itself, makes awareness expand, grow, and become stronger. That which you concentrate on lights up. When conscious awareness ceases to light up things outside of you and turns inward and shines upon the light already within you, it produces such incredibly strong power you are able to break through the illusion you are just a body. In the end, there is nothing but Light and Consciousness reflecting Light and Consciousness. But you have to focus your awareness on the Light within, doing it over and over again. This is where your will power can help. You must continuously take your awareness off the 'outside' world and focus it inside, where you know the Light resides, and then wait for it to manifest.

1.3 You Are Already Enlightened

My friends, you are always aware. You don't wake up in the morning and say, "Am I here? Am I alive?" Awareness is always present—always. In the midst of insanity, a really good therapist knows one basic truth. No matter how chaotic and diffused the consciousness, there is still a central core of personality. There has to be a place where consciousness is totally compact, totally present. It is a point of inner integration and the therapist keeps the person going back to where they can feel that presence. There is always a sense of 'I.' "I am insane. I am desperate. I am out of control." 'I' is always present.

Your body would explode into separate particles if conscious awareness were not intensely present in the physical. No matter what the chaotic state, whether insanity, addiction or anything in between, when a therapist perseveres, they can find a place where the person has a sense of themselves, as 'I.' Any time you go inside with your awareness, looking for awareness and nothing else, you will find it, without words, without form, without shape, without idea. It is the 'I' of the 'I am.' That's what I mean by focusing awareness on itself.

Ramana Maharshi* says, "Who am I?" Go around all day asking, "Who am I?" meaning, "I want to feel that point of conscious awareness that is the 'I' of me, the single I." When you start asking the question, "Who am I?" or simply go within and drift down into it, you shine the light of consciousness upon itself and all the magic of that alchemy begins to be felt. Turning lead into gold is nothing compared to this. If you can turn lead into gold, you can turn gold into lead, and who cares? But to take the light of consciousness and turn it on itself, will make the truth of what is really present felt and known. When you are aware of its presence within you, *that is illumination.*

This is the highest teaching I can give you. The job is simple. If you want to know who you are, take the initiative, go within and feel your own conscious awareness over and over again. You are seeking that which you already are. "The greatest obstacle to your illumination is the belief that you are not already illumined." Ramana said it. What does this mean? It means you are *already* illuminated, and that illumination is always present. So you see the frustration because you are trying to find out who you are, believing that who you are is not who you are. This creates confusion, and the way out is to go inside yourself with the *intention* of feeling who you are. Go past the thoughts and emotions to the ever-present witness that passes through your mind, your emotions and your body. It is the 'I' of you, it is your awareness.

The manifest world of form, thought and emotion appears

to be very real, doesn't it? The challenge is to test this 'fact.' Every time you have a thought, ask yourselves if it is connected to the eternal, or is it hooked up to something that is not going to last. Your body is an excellent laboratory for this because a great percentage of your thoughts are connected to the idea that you are a body. With examination, you will come to understand that any thought which has to do with your body is not eternal because you know full well your body is going to dissolve. So why not just think God-thoughts? Because *thinking* God without feeling God can be as boring as thinking grocery lists. God is not a thought, God is a feeling.

1.4 The Psyche Yearns For Wholeness

Your psyche is spherical, whole and complete. When you are approaching an experience of that wholeness, you begin to notice circles and spheres. The sun and moon are magnificent spherical mandalas, and isn't it a wonderful gift that both by day and by night, the heavens present the symbol of your wholeness to you. I have never seen a drawing or painting of an enlightened one with a square around their head instead of a halo. All the great mandalas are spherical. If you were able to slow down every scene of your nightly dreams, you would find a sphere or circle somewhere within each frame of them. The sphere contains the center point of your cohesive power. It can be used as another imaging device to aid in your movement toward wholeness. Just stop once in awhile and visualize a sphere within you, then go on about your business. The part of your spherical psyche beneath conscious awareness that recognizes this symbol wants integration, and will then help the process. When you begin to meditate, just sit and breathe, then imagine in your mind a sphere or a circle anywhere within you. It can be of light or of emptiness. The psyche will know you are turning toward that point of unity within, and it will do everything it can to bring you to that place. Your job is to concentrate on the inner sphere, and drop to the place within where you feel most comfortable, then extend your awareness into it.

Please, feel the ease of this gentle extending. Don't make it complicated. Complication separates. Worry separates. If you are spending time worrying, *worry* is what will manifest. Concentrate upon what is eternal, such as the sphere of light within, and enlightenment will come forward. There is only one thing you can say that is eternally true about yourself, and that is you exist. The feeling-tone that is you goes on throughout all the stages of your beingness from birth to death. It never changes. So concentrate on that sense, and awaken.

1.5 Allowing Bliss

Someone asked why I brought you to Hawaii. You will find, if you have not found out already, it is very difficult to keep from relaxing in Hawaii. The soft motion of this lovely place is very soothing. It doesn't remind you of Taos, Detroit or New York. I asked you to come here because when you leave your own environment and place yourself in one where you have very few responsibilities, you begin to let go. You begin to allow yourself to move toward your bliss. You have no responsibilities except to be here and use this time. That's why we travel. All you need to do is 'be' and let things happen, let things explode, let clarity come. You can pick up the rest of your life when you get back on the airplane. With this kind of simplicity, we can accomplish many things. You have these days to do nothing else but concentrate on awakening to the memory of who you have always been. So let it happen. The concentration, gentle, yet firm, is essential.

1.6 Mountains and Monkeys

Many of you fault yourselves because you are not consistently loving. You feel the rise and fall of loving feelings. Perhaps it will help if I remind you again that your ego is not capable of consistent love. It doesn't want to be consistently loving because it enjoys moving between polarities. You don't take a monkey and make it into a mountain. A monkey is a monkey and will move from tree to tree. A mountain is a mountain and will maintain itself as mountain. Your ego is the monkey, your Self is the mountain. The monkey running all over the mountain does not change the essence of mountain, does it? Mountain stays mountain. Monkeys do what they do. They fight, they scream, they make love, they live, they die, they eat bananas. And this does not change the essence of the mountain upon which they perform all their actions. You can choose to use monkey mind or feel mountain.

You need to identify and realign with mountain because that is what is really here. *Mountain*, not monkeys. They are very different things, and they *feel* very different. The more you fall into the mountain of your Being, of awareness, and the more you turn the light of that awareness on itself, the stronger it becomes.

1.7 The Delight Of The Physical

All of the struggle toward consciousness takes place in the physical body. Because you have been trained to keep your attention *away* from body-sensations and body-awareness, you are missing the incredible, empowering energy that moves through it. You no longer experience the legitimate delight of feeling all the different parts of your Wholeness moving through you. And because you do not feel what is inside you, you have cut yourself off from feeling the Presence of God. God is an energy field of alive, conscious awareness, pulsating and singing with life force through your Wholeness—and your body is part of that Wholeness.

Many of you are hanging on hoping you will get through this life without really feeling. You are afraid that when you start to feel, you will feel your guilt, your losses, death, pain and tears, all the anguish you have tried to avoid. But I have told you from the very beginning, be careful about not wanting to feel. The spigot is either on or it's off, and if it's off, you are not going to allow yourself to feel *anything*. But if you are willing to feel fully, now, marvelous things can happen. Yes, some of the painful feelings will arise, but so will the exhilarating bliss of God and I assure you, it is worth the risk.

My friends, please hear me: *You are Light. You come from Light, you will always be an extension of Light.* You have no form unless you choose to move into form. As Light, you are omniscient and omnipresent. There is nothing you need because you are the All. Your purity of consciousness moves and joins with the rest of the One. You are limitless in the boundlessness of creation. There is no place that is not your home because everywhere there is but Light. So wherever you go, you will simply find yourself, manifesting again and again and yet again, pushing past all limits of mind into pure, spontaneous creation. The small, limited self dies before the expansive explosion of your Being. You are pure Self, pure Consciousness, pure Light, moving through all of the past and the future. That is what you are. You have never been anything else, you can never be anything else. You and the Source are One. All separation is illusion. So know your Self and be free.

2.1 Who Am I?

What I would like to work on today is how to help you access the level of your consciousness that contains such things as peace, light, liberation, love, total awareness and total acceptance. It's necessary to learn how to do this because, unless you find a way to access this level consciously a few times every hour of the day, you will never really gain the momentum necessary to move you into your own awakening.

A very interesting event happened recently which can be of help in building your momentum. A gentleman came to visit and we had a private exchange. It was clear he was dying and also very clear he was dying of AIDS. I have worked with AIDS people before, but there was something different about this man. There

was very little *guilt* in his aura. He had managed to move from
guilt-ridden victim/victimizer into a space that contained some
fear, but most of all a lot of excitement about the next stage of his
unfoldment. I asked him how he had come to this expanded peace
with the ability to be so free.

He told me he had been travelling alone in a foreign country
and had become ill. He was diagnosed as having AIDS. The first
two weeks after the diagnosis were as close to hell as anything he
had ever experienced. For those weeks, he was too frightened to
eat, too anxious to sleep, and felt constantly lonely and lost. What
circumstances had done was to put him through two weeks of
rigorous austerities and renunciations, paring away all the non-
essentials, and leaving only the bare bones of his dilemma.

One night, he suddenly realized it came down to a simple
question of what he was going to believe. He was either guilty and
therefore karmically or morally deserving of illness, or he was
innocent. That was the only question to be settled. Innocence or
guilt. He went deeply into his being looking for this guilty
person, the bad boy, the one who should be punished—but he
could not find him. There was only one thing he *could* find—
consciousness moving through life choices the best way he could,
doing his utmost to have integrity with himself and others at
every moment, not hiding from himself, not pretending and not
posturing. Given who he was and what he knew, he had done his
best to be harmless. He had made his choices moment by
moment, using as much wisdom as he possessed. He had done
the best he could under all the circumstances of his life. Upon
looking within, all he could find was innocence. And in that
moment, he was free of guilt.

It's very simple, my friends. Either you are guilty as charged
by all the rules of religion and society, or you are innocent, and
that is what we are here to decide today. These rules and restrictions which make you feel guilty, push you to the place where you
have to grapple with the same question this gentleman had to

face. Either you are innocent or you are guilty. And who must decide? You! Your *mind* will give you good reasons to maintain both positions, so thoughts are no help. What does help is connecting with the part of yourself that bypasses your mental ledger sheet and *knows who you are*. That part of you knows your basic nature is innocent.

Nothing outside of yourself can give you an explanation that releases you from this quest. Your Being is the only place to find your freedom, your release. When you find yourself *totally* innocent and realize your innocence is held deeply inside you, God-Awareness is right behind. You must find that place of total, innocent purity. You are pure, conscious awareness. The first word is no mistake. Purity is an energy, alive inside your consciousness, in your body, now!

To find that energy, we begin by loosening the binds that hold you to ego. One of those is the underlying belief that you are a body. You are not a body. You are pure, conscious awareness manifesting in all things, and connected intimately with the Source that gave rise to your consciousness. You are as your Creator created you and your Creator is not a body. Much of your confusion and immersion in guilt come from the misidentification of what you are. If you are talking about your body, the words that come out of your mouth, the actions your body performs, then you cannot escape the fact you have done things with them that have harmed others. Is there anyone who can deny this is true? If you are a body, if you are these actions, if you are those words, if that is who you are, then you stand guilty. But what if you are *not* that? If you are innocent of these charges, your liberation will come as you begin to identify with what you *really* are.

Your mind tries to bring about some kind of karmic payoff due from all the damage your body, mind and mouth have caused. If you look closely, you will find every so-called 'harmful act' you have ever committed can be traced back to a place within you that felt you as a body needed to do certain things in order to be safe. Therein lies your difficulty because you have misidentified again. *You will never be safe as a body.* How can you be safe as a body? The body is under attack all the time. You can walk out your door and in five minutes be dead on the street! Where can you find safety in the ever-changing world of bodies? Identify with your body, and you will constantly be filled with fear.

What you have done you can undo. Since there really is no such thing as time-space, it can also be done in a moment. Misidentification comes from thinking yourself to be something you are not and then believing it. You feel guilty about the acts you have performed under that misidentification. But in truth, when a consciousness is filled with fear, it will do anything it can to protect itself. The only way to have harmlessness alive on this planet is for the majority of you to stop feeling afraid. When you no longer feel fear, you no longer have the need to attack others in order to assure your safety. But as things are now, you have fear, and that makes your love unreliable. Fear produces attack. Love produces harmony. As you move between these two, you are always afraid, afraid of harming others and being harmed yourself. That is the reality of the fear-separated consciousness. Until mankind finds a way to break out of fear, you will go on harming and being harmed. There is no blame for that pattern. How can you be blamed when you are motivated out of a sense of terror?

What is needed is to be constant in your love. You will never be a consistently loving consciousness until you are safe, and you will never be safe until you go to the only place where safety lies, which is in the Heart of God. Safety is found there and no place else. You will never talk yourself into loving kindness. You cannot. It is an experience that builds in you, day after day. You have got to make the decision to experience that feeling. Make the decision now and it will begin to unfold as you return over and over to the Heart of God.

2.2 The Heart of God

The 'Heart of God' is that place within you which is connected deeply with the source of Love itself. Learn to immerse
yourself in that center of awareness and allow its energy to
transform your fears into safety. You have the responsibility of
making your way into your own 'heart.' I do not mean into your
solar plexus, which is the seat of conditional love, nor do I mean
your physical heart. I am talking about a place of awareness deep
within you. Some find it in the heart chakra area. Others find it 'in
their mind.' Some see it, others feel it. It is the seat of awareness in
you and it will reveal itself.

The energy to move you to that loving kindness is available
when you drop into your 'heart' a hundred times, a thousand
times, ten thousand times, as you move away from the world of
change into that which is changeless. You will never, ever be free
until you know that. You can become as 'holy' as you want, you
can guard your words, you can guard your actions, but you
cannot guard your mind. And it is the mind that creates your
world.

The Heart of God is not metaphorical. It is pure, conscious
awareness. It is a reality and Its energy can be felt within you.
Immersed in that Source, you will realize you are not afraid. As
you identify who you are more and more with this Source, you
begin to feel your harmlessness. You will no longer feel fear. And
you will do no harm if you are not afraid.

2.3 You Are Not Who You Think You Are

We have stated that the problem presented is to decide who
you are. And is who you are innocent, or are you guilty? In order
to help facilitate that understanding, it would be extremely helpful for you to be aware of who you think you are right now. You
carry various views of yourself around that your conscious mind
may not be aware of. Nevertheless, whether you are aware of them
or not, you act out of those views.

Let us begin to clarify who you think you are by having you take up paper and pencil and define yourself on it. There are many parts to you. You have a body and you think you are the body, and you think you are the things your body does. You have emotions and you think you are the emotions that you display. You have a mind and you think you are those thoughts. So, please put down all definitions of yourself and please do it in the following format: "I am..." "I am an angry person." "I am a jealous person." "I am a sexually harmful person." "I am a deprived person." "I am a lonely person." "I am an intelligent person." "I am a stupid person." "I am an unhealthy person." "I am a loving person." And on and on. Please note that there are contradictions. It is absolutely possible for you to think that, on the one hand, you are a loving person, and on the other, to think you are harmful. It is possible to think you are kind and that you are unkind. Allow yourself to put down all of these varying views of yourself. Take as long as you need to prepare this list, because it is important.

Pause until completed.

Now let us examine the list. You will notice it defines you in a way that necessitates having a body. For example, if you say you are loving, this means you are loving to someone. If you say you are honest, it assumes you are honest to someone about something. In fact, as you go down the list, which I ask you to do now, please note carefully that in all of your identifications, there is an assumption that there is a separate you, an 'I' that is separated from other. And even more important, please note how many of these identifications rest upon some form of identification with your body.

I am trying to undermine your belief that a separated body-self is you. What you have written on your list requires that body-self be present in order to do anything or to be anything on your list. What I want you to see is that, if you cross off everything which has to do with this separated you, you will end up with nothing. Yet, if you are asked, you would certainly say you exist, that there is a 'you,' an 'I,' that exists. You would say, "But I am."

Who is this 'I' that remains? If you say, "I am determined to find God," the minute that you say 'I' and 'God,' you are talking about a 'you' that has to go somewhere and find something. We are back to our list. *The part of you that wants to find God, that yearns to go Home, is the part that still believes there is a separated you that has someplace to go and something to do.* It is that part which believes you are a thing or a form. You are not a 'thing.' You are not a 'form.' If you are not all of those things, if you do not have a form, then *who are you?* Are you nothing? No. But you are no-thing. I am asking you to quit defining yourself as something and begin to define yourself as no-thing. It is not easy.

This is a steep path. There has to be a constant realization that those things you have identified yourself with, are confused about, are embroiled in, are addicted to, are *not* who you are. If you pay attention to this, the way will become clear. For example, you find yourself in a state of anger. You have already found out you are not anger because it takes 'someone' to be angry. So, the question is, "*Who* is angry?" You find yourself hungry. You say, "*Who* is hungry?" You find yourself bored. "*Who* is bored?" You find yourself in fear. "*Who* is afraid?" Go back to the original question, over and over again.

It is important to understand that you don't answer the question because the question cannot be answered in the usual way. You wait until the question begins to answer itself. It will answer through a 'knowing,' not a 'thinking.' This process is one of constantly turning the spotlight of awareness back on the 'I,' the Self, and the Self will reveal Itself. Again and again. Is it tedious? Perhaps for some at the beginning, but to reap the harvest of knowing *who you are* is worth everything.

So we go back to our original dilemma—are you guilty? Innocent? You are wedged into a terrible position. But *who* is wedged? *Who* is guilty? *Who* is innocent? Do not answer. Stop and allow. Fall into that internal place where all answers come from and wait.

2.4 Guilt Is A Messenger

Let us examine deeply this concept of guilt. If you look with care at those things you feel guilty about, you will find they have to do with form. You never go around feeling guilty because you love God, or because you are pure, conscious awareness. You feel guilty about actions, thoughts, responses and beliefs that arise out of your absolute dedication to the thought that you are a form of some kind. And if you are feeling guilty, you are suffering.

What do you believe about suffering? On examination, you will find that many of you believe that suffering brings God-Consciousness. It is true that God-Consciousness *can* come through suffering, but it doesn't *have to*. A messenger knocks on the door and gives you a message. Does he come in, sit down and stay with you for fifteen years? No, he delivers the message and leaves. Suffering is a messenger, delivering the message that says, "Wake up to what's going on! If I, Suffering, am present, it means awakening is needed. Wake up!" Then Suffering goes on to say, "Will you use me to awaken or have I awakened you by my knocking? Can you awaken to the knowing of how to rest in your inner being, seeking love through comfort, without the pressure of my presence? Can I leave now?" Guilt, like suffering, is just a knock, but a very loud one. There are other ways knocking can be heard. Asking, "Who Am I?" is one such way.

2.5 An Exercise in Awareness

I would like to present a short exercise to aid you in this process of asking, "Who am I?" Please find a partner to work with. We shall call you person A and the other, person B. Person A starts making verbal statements about themselves. He or she may begin by telling person B the story of their life, or what they had to eat this morning, or where they bought the pair of shoes on their feet. Person B, meanwhile, sits quietly, with eyes closed, listening carefully. After person A says, for example, "I was born in California," person B says quietly, gently and out loud, "Who was born in California?" As each statement is given, as each main idea is completed, such as, "I had a very difficult time in my early years," person B replies, "Who had a difficult time?" Person A says, "I went to kindergarten when I was four years old." "Who went to kindergarten? Who was four years old?" This kind of response is made after every single identification. Then, both A and B simply sit with the question, "Who?" for just a moment, and then go on with their story.

It helps to set a time limit, let us say, thirty seconds, for person A to speak and to be questioned, then it switches to person B. If you find thirty seconds is not enough, extend it to a time you feel works best for you. The point of this exercise is to help each other get into the mental habit of asking after segments of thought, "Who had the thought? Who experienced that? Who is thinking that? Who is afraid of this?" It is essential you realize that as you ask the question, what you want is to get an instant feeling of going inside and waiting. Some part of you knows who you really are, aside from all the ideas and all the beliefs about who you are. This process is one of knowing and waiting quietly inside in perfect trust that you can find out who you are. Try to feel, not think. Feel that place within you. Feel that 'I' within. Practice.

Pause until finished.

If you have another method that keeps you totally present and immersed in the feeling of the moment, use it. If "Who am I?" separates you from the moment, don't use it—just stay in the moment. Do whatever you want, but bring yourself into the moment so you can be aware of all that is going on in it. If you enjoy being half asleep, then stay half asleep. But if you want to really feel the force of life, you have to find a way to awaken to it, because it is only in the moment of 'now' that true Life can be experienced.

A final technique for those of you dealing with guilt is this. When the guilty thought arises, step back to the level of saying, "Who's feeling this guilt? Who's feeling anxious?" And then just wait for the response. It is out of the immersion into who you really are that the joy of being arises. "Who Am I?" makes you conscious of the stepping back, away from the false. It takes the pressure off having to make all those small mind decisions about who you are. It's a falling back into your 'being.' You are absolute, perfect, aware consciousness manifesting now, so relax and enjoy it. Relax and experience it, that's all we're asking. You will find when you really experience who you are, you are *not guilty*. Your mind condemns you, but the 'I' will not.

Please, be present in your life, feel it, be aware of your thoughts, aware of your feelings, and also aware of *who* is doing it all anyway. *You don't know who you are.* You have defined yourselves by attributes that will be meaningless the minute you leave your body. All points of reference for who you are will be gone. People die in confusion because they have identified so completely with their physical, mental and emotional selves. When they no longer have them, *then* they ask, "Who am I?" Ask it now so you will begin to know you are pure, conscious, aware Light that is experienced as total Love and total acceptance. All the rest are like the images on a movie screen. They come and go, but the screen remains the same. You can have images of hellfire and brimstone, but they don't affect the screen. You can have pictures of God-Consciousness, Christ and Buddha, and they *still* don't affect the screen. The screen is the Eternal, the Changeless, the Real. All images play upon it, but it does not change. So identify with the eternal screen of your Being. It will give you safety, which will allow you to totally relax into the moment, and be totally open to Life.

3.1 Love Is In Your Heart

The path I have been presenting these days is not the only way to find God. It is simply the fast path, in other words, it is the direct climb up the mountain. I present it because I have an increasing sense that some of you really want to get on with it. You are no longer content to merely read and think and hope, but want to merge with your experiences rather than continuously having to seek to find them. You wish to move from the position of the seeker and to be definitely on the road as finder. To do that, you must be able to take what is usually on the periphery of your awareness and concentrate on it. In order to really experience one's Being requires a willingness to continually concentrate the energy of your awareness here in the moment.

One such way is through the heart center. The heart center is a wellspring of undifferentiated love to which you have total access at any moment. It is undifferentiated in the sense that the heart does not have any particular thing or any one person it loves more than any other. When you begin to immerse yourself in the heart center, the feeling of love increases almost instantly. The delightful thing about this particular approach is the gradual feeling of expansion around the boundaries of your love patterns. You will honestly find yourself feeling love in the most astonishing moments. You're sitting on a subway reaching for the stillness within when someone with a very loud ghetto blaster sits down in the seat opposite you. Suddenly you feel this upwelling inside and you realize it's love. And who is the object of the love? The person with the ghetto blaster.

It's this kind of surprise that comes into one's consciousness, totally unbidden, and sweeps over you without calling up any particular person outside of oneself. As this happens time after time, you become more attracted to this undifferentiated love, which is the most magnetic force in the world. It is not true that differentiated love conquers all. Differentiated love gets you into a lot of humbug. It makes you and other people miserable. But when you get in the realm of undifferentiated, spontaneously combustible love energy, it is as though you become magnetized and you are pulled to that place more and more.

As with any two magnets which have their fields lined up, there is a point where they attract each other to such an extent that they come together without any more effort. The two magnets are your awareness and the love within the heart center. It's not very difficult to do. It's like a sweet dropping, experiencing and drifting of your awareness deeply down inside yourself for a few moments with the total expectation the sweetness of that undifferentiated Light and Love is going to manifest.

So the approach is twofold. Just as you are immersed more deeply into the sense of love, at the same time, the sense of 'Who Am I' brings you to the clarity of total wisdom as well. So, pause awhile in the feeling of the heart center, just a gentle placing of awareness, letting go of the external and resting there. The rest of the time, when you are out in the world, keep the conscious question going of 'who is living this'?

3.2 The Illusion of Time and Space

Let me explain what I mean when I say there is no such thing as time and space. Once you break out of the energy vibration of this planet by deepening your consciousness to a vibrational level beyond it, you will find everything happening at once. Your mind cannot fully understand this phenomenon until you experience it. As long as you believe there is such a thing as progress, you will believe in time. My words are as wind when you are using the brain of the human, physical apparatus because it is constructed in such a way as to make the linear progression of time and space a reality to you. You have all made an agreement, coming into earth plane consciousness, that you will pretend there are such things as time, space, progress and decay. Totally immersed in this agreement, it is very real to you.

All this wonderful drama you have created as human separated consciousness goes on and as long as you stay on that frequency, you will believe it and experience progress. But please understand, since this is a planet of polarity, if there is progress there has to be its opposite. There must be regression. What you create here must die here. But there is a level beyond this one where all polarity is seen for exactly what it is, which is the rising and falling of limited awareness. Grounded deeply beneath and around these limitations there is something quite different going on, from which all this illusion is allowed. Human consciousness plays out the drama of pitter-patter up the ladder. Well, eventually there comes a moment when you realize you and the ladder and the space around it are all One. There is no place to go, nothing to do—except to experience What Is!

Progress equals expectation of a specific kind. Progress is the expectation of doing better, and with it comes the deep fear that you are not going to do better. I know I am asking you to pull yourselves out of lifetimes of belief patterns, and I realize how difficult it is, but you can do it. You do it by asking the question, "Who am I?" and by going to that place where unconditional love is present. Then you simply wait with an expectation that is an invitation to experience what you are looking for.

3.3 Looking In The Wrong Place

One of the things that kills your spontaneous joy in life is the constant judgmental critique you have running against yourself. You have no idea the number of moments you spend criticizing your looks, your diet, your friendships, your speech, your house, your car, your job, etc., etc. *In order to really understand what I mean, I would like you to take a few moments to write down all of the judgments that, **one**, you have against yourself, and **two**, you think the world holds about you. Please be very specific and thorough in recording these.*

Pause.

Alright, my friends, let me tell you what your list represents. It represents a great deal of energy drain and it represents a tremendous amount of defensive awareness. When you are still trying to please the world or to have the world find you pleasing, you are trapped in this downward spiraling energy vortex. You will constantly be trying to assess how well you are doing, constantly ruminating about how to appear in order to get what you want or to please others. In the end, my friends, the only thing that brings you the love you are looking for in this world, is the love in you. And that love is already there, in perfect safety and wholeness. You do not have to create the love—just allow yourself to experience it.

You are trying to get love using the wrong technique. The point here is very simple. Everyone wants to feel loved, and every one of you wants to feel love. You believe it takes someone outside yourself who miraculously happens to 'love' you, to feel loved. So you spend your lives looking for this someone. But in the deepest part of you, you are not trying to find someone to love you, you are trying to feel love within yourself. And your list of judgments, however subtle, comes in to undercut all your awareness of the love that is within you.

Again, we end up where we always do, which is, the way to have your life filled with love and to feel in a state of love, is to begin, now, to be still and go to the place where love has its home. Love has its home *within your body*. In your physical body, there is a true connection, a real, honest to God doorway within the heart chakra that will release this incredible, unending supply of love you want so much to feel in your world. The only remaining difficulty to overcome is for you to truly let yourself know you must stop looking outside yourself. Just stop, and in that action of dropping deeply into your Being, you build a new energy vortex you can use to remove those things from your life which no longer delight you and add those things you have deeply yearned for.

3.4 Making Creative Movements In Your Life

You weren't sent to the earth plane as a punishment. You were sent here to enjoy it, to delight in it, to have a life that makes you jump out of bed in the morning instead of pulling the covers over your head. Make up your mind to find those places in your life that are not giving you spontaneous excitement and be responsible for replacing them with things that do delight you.

If your life doesn't have some aspects of deep creativity in it, I will assure you that you are not as happy as you could be. I do not say you have to be the greatest artist in town or the greatest dancer in the state. The point here is, if you do not *consciously* have a place in your life where you are creative and dynamic, you are not going to feel whole. It is the releasing of the creative energy within you that is important. The energy needs to move. I am talking about making creative movements in the energy around you so you can open up new parts of your life. No matter what your life is like, when you begin to release the creative energy waiting there, you will also begin to feel life more deeply. The creative pursuit in itself is not important. It is the releasing of energy into something you want to do that makes you feel delight and excitement.

When you begin to get a taste of it, you will yearn for more. Your responsibility is to be dynamic, creative human beings, expressing this pure, conscious awareness in whatever way makes your life begin to explode. It doesn't matter what your age, explosion is explosion. I have seen people in their seventies so full of exploding power and wonder that to see them psychically, they could be twenty-five. And I have seen twenty-five year olds so imploded, they could be at the end of their lives. It has to do with deciding you want to enjoy life.

My friends, life is a process. You do not have to know where the end is going to be. And you don't have to start worrying about having to give up one thing to do another. Your responsibility is not to pick and choose. Your responsibility is to find within yourself those things you feel would make your life explosive, alive and full. Then it is up to your destiny, to your energies, to your wholeness of Being, to manifest them in ways that are harmless and maximum for everyone. I told you before, God has no favorites. God will not pick you over someone else, or some-one else over you. You can be your creative self without harming others. God and you will find a way.

If your real determination is to release the energy you have

been sitting on, as you do, you will begin to feel differently about
yourself. Please start doing something *for yourself,* not to please
others, just for yourself. Commit to that and the energy will build
and spread into ever increasing areas of consciousness. The way
will show you the way. You do not have to know the five-year plan
for your consciousness. All you need is your assessment of the
present condition, of those things you would love to have
changed, and what kind of feeling-tone you would like to have in
its place. If you don't take the time to clarify those things for
yourself, you will be at a standstill.

I am not talking about a job, whether to move, what kind of
house you should buy or should you buy a car. I am talking about
making a commitment to change, the kind of change which
explodes in a new way. Keep your eyes open and it *will* start to
happen. The universe is totally on your side and is filling you full
of information all the time. You are not a closed system. This earth
plane is filled with information for all of you, so listen. I am
asking you to move into new parts of your being. Move energy on
any level and it will move on all levels. The outside and the inside
are not separate. Make a move on the outside, even a small one,
and your being will get the message you are breaking down the
old and building new awareness. Don't try to outguess God. Just
know the things that will make you exuberantly happy, alive and
grounded. Discover them with trust in the universe and watch
what happens.

3.5 Find Yourself And Be Free

Let us go back to the topic we were talking about on the first
day we gathered. I asked you to recognize that you carry a feeling
of guilt for having been able to manifest your kind of life, with the
free time, the adequate finances, and the willingness of others to
allow you to come here to find God. But it is true those who do
not have to worry about their next meal or how to keep from
being killed have an excellent opportunity to find God. Much of

this planet is under incredible stress merely trying to live through the day, and find enough to eat to keep any kind of consciousness alive.

Your life is not like that. Most of your worries, compared to a great many on this planet, are much less intense. That is *not* something to feel guilty about. It is a reason for gratitude, and a reason for asking yourself why you have been given this opportunity, and what your responsibility around it is. *Move into the world of light and pure consciousness as far as you possibly can and it will benefit the entire planet.* I will tell you this—they need your help.

Those of you who have the awareness and the opportunity to help, I beg you to do it. Find your light, find your love, find your clarity, find out who you are. You are in a perfect position. If you cannot do it for yourself, do it for others because we all need your help. Turn on the television any day and you will sense what I am talking about. Don't spend an ounce of energy feeling guilty. Just say, "Thank you and I intend to use it to bring as much light, love, compassion and understanding onto this planet as I possibly can." Those of you who are awakening, that is the job. Everything else is secondary.

By the grace of God and your own hard work, some of you are on the verge of real understanding, of really knowing who you are. Don't stop. Don't get caught up in the mundane. Don't get trapped by your petty problems. Just keep remembering there is a job to do and it is to increase your joy, your love, your light, and your dance of delight. To any extent you can bring delight into the living process of this planet, you are helping those who at this moment do not have the foggiest notion such a thing is possible.

I beg you, not one moment of feeling guilty. That's wasting time. That's ego talking. I came here to remind you that you are here to love, and to experience your own Being which is love. You are here to explode the light of pure consciousness in and around you. You are here to know that *all pain is illusion* and with that knowledge you will benefit millions. So if you want to help, find your light, find yourself, find your God, and be free.

---

*Ramana Maharshi (1879-1950) was the guru who refused to be regarded as a guru, much as Socrates was the sage whose only claim to knowledge was his own ignorance. Ramana relentlessly urged the seeker to find out *who* is seeking, who is asking the question. He stated time and again that the greatest obstacle to Realization is the belief that the seeker is unrealized. The issue is to find out *who* believes he or she is unenlightened (and if this seems too rigorous, the question becomes: To *whom* is this too rigorous?).

Ramana answers the question "Who am I?" metaphorically. He says we experience life like a motion picture, captivated by the images moving across the screen, while ignoring the fact that our True Self is the screen upon which the images are cast. We don't have to go anywhere or do anything to become the Self, we ARE the Self, upon which the drama of life is reflected.

He also talks about waking, dreaming, and the deep sleep (the last of which most closely approximates the experience of the Self.)

A devotee came with a question: Since individual souls and Brahman are one, what is the cause of this creation (the manifest world)?

M: *The object of creation is to remove the confusion of your individuality. The question shows that you have identified yourself with the body and therefore see yourself and the world around. You think that you are the body. Your mind and intellect are the factors of your wrong identity.*

Do you exist in your sleep?

D: I do.

M: *The same being is now awake and asks these questions. Is it so?*

D: Yes.

M: *These questions did not arise in your sleep. Did they?*

D: No.

M: *Why not? Because you did not see your body and no thoughts arose. You did not identify yourself with the body then. Therefore these questions did not arise.*

They arise now because of your identity with the body. Is it not so?

D: Yes.

M: *Now see which is your real nature. Is it that which is free from thoughts or that which is full of thoughts?*

Being is continuous. The thoughts are discontinuous. So which is permanent?

D: Being.

M: *That is it. Realize it. That is your true nature. Your nature is simple Being, free from thoughts.*

Because you identify yourself with the body you want to know about creation. The world and the objects including your body appear in the waking state but disappear in the state of sleep. You exist all through these states. Find it out. That is your Self.

D: Supposing it is found, what then?

M: *Find it out and see. There is no use asking hypothetical questions.*

D: Am I then one with Brahman?

M: *Leave Brahman alone. Find out who you are. Brahman can take care of Himself.*

If you cease to identify yourself with the body no questions regarding creation, birth, death, etc., will arise. They did not arise in your sleep. Similarly they will not arise in the true state of the Self.

The object of creation is thus clear, that you should proceed from where you find yourself and realize your true being.[1]

M: *Our very experience of the **jagrat** (waking) and the **swapna** (dream) states proves that the Consciousness as the Self underlies all...states, remains perfect all along and witnesses all of them. But with regard to similar consciousness in the deep sleep, every person is known to say "I was not aware of anything; I slept sound and happily". Two facts emerge from the statement (unawareness of anything and the* *happiness of sound sleep). Unless these existed and were experienced in sleep they could not find expression by the same person in the waking state. Inference also leads to the same conclusion. Just as the eye sees the darkness which remains enveloping all objects, so also the Self sees the darkness of nescience which remained covering the phenomenal world.*

This darkness was experienced when it (the Self) emerged in dots of supreme bliss, shone a trice and fleeted away in such fine subtlety as the rays of the moon which peer through the waving foliage. The experience was however not through any media (such as the senses or the mind), but bears out the fact that consciousness does exist in deep sleep. The unawareness is owing to the absence of relative knowledge, and the happiness to the absence of (seething) thoughts.

*If the experience of bliss in deep sleep is a fact, how is it that no one among all the human beings recollects it? A diver who has found the desired thing under water cannot make his discovery known to the expectant persons on the shore until he emerges from the water. Similarly the sleeper cannot express his experience because he cannot contact the organs of expression until he is awakened by his **vasanas** (latent tendencies) in due course. Therefore it follows that the Self is the light of Sat (Existence), Chit (Consciousness), Ananda (Bliss).* [2]

As Ramana lay dying (April 14, 1950), devotees were overcome with despair. They begged him not to leave them. With compassion and bliss in his eyes, he responded, "I am not going away. Where could I go? I am here."

At the moment of death, a bright meteor was seen all over South India, moving slowly from south to north. Members of the ashram saw it disappear behind Arunachala, the sacred mountain. Ramana, the steadfast guru who was not a guru, had come home.—*Justin Moore*

---

[1] Talks with Sri Ramana Maharshi, *Sri Ramanashramam, Tiruvannamalai, S. India, 1968, pp. 566-567.*

[2] Ibid., *pp. 580-581.*

ENERGY, MIRACLES AND GODDESSES

March 19, 1989
Albuquerque, New Mexico

E
L
D
E
R

B
R
O
T
H
E
R

59

Many of you have been working for years to raise your level of consciousness and I know there are times when the job seems too difficult. But I want to encourage you in your endeavors by reminding you of the very wise choice you made to incarnate at the present time. It is wise because moving over the earth plane is a vast new source of energy, and since the energy is real, the acceleration of power here is also real.

You have been asking for such things as courage, strength, enlightenment, wisdom, love and understanding, and when you ask with a deep inner longing, the unseen world does respond. This is not just a figment of the mind, or a fragment of hope, it is a reality. The true desire of your heart goes out and the unseen world rushes to maximize that energy flow for you. I know many have hoped it would come as a dramatic surge of power instantly felt, which in turn would let you know you have been doing a good job of awakening. But please realize, if you were to feel the power full-force and all at once, many difficulties would arise. The energy is sent in increments, and force and power are regulated, thus making it possible for you to gradually absorb this new energy into the cellular structures of your body.

As with any new surge of power into a specific form, things

can get out of balance until one becomes accustomed to it. You might experience depression, when you haven't been depressed for years, or physical things such as headaches or short-lived, unusual illnesses. You might be irritable, or feel the desire to change when there is nothing obvious for you to change into. You might even begin to feel differently about parts of your lives you have never questioned. Our response is, please be patient. Let it be. Just keep feeling and experiencing the energy as it comes in with as much humor as possible, allowing it to make its slow, careful and balanced adjustment in your life.

When energy moves into the physical body, it runs into old patterns within the cells themselves, and it is through the gentle action of the energy acting on cells, emotions and mind, that changes are going to come about. The buffeting of new energy breaks loose the old and allows the new to take form. It's obvious this process can in some periods be uncomfortable, because it is difficult to let go of the old when the new is not yet firmly in place. Become aware of your body, your emotions, your belief structures and your thoughts, exactly as they are, and then imagine a new, rejuvenating energy field coming from the Vast Source of the Deep Self permeating all of them. The changes will come. Remind the cells that relaxation is the way to expansion. When you feel your emotions tighten up, just remind yourself that relaxation around those emotions is what brings the greatest relief. If your mind gets tense over certain thoughts and you gnaw on those thoughts like a dog on a bone, tell your mind to relax, to let things go, and you will find a general state of well-being will come upon you.

To help with this process, I would suggest you increase the number of times during the day when you quiet down and allow yourself to consciously remember this energy is present. When you increase the number of times you do this, or extend your one meditation period, you will be able to feel the changes. Make sure to go into the mental, emotional and physical *feelings* with the awareness that things are being changed and transmuted. As you participate more deeply with this process and become more familiar with it, you will be much less likely to have times of depression, confusion, or a sense of being off balance. The more familiar you are with the energy, the more you keep it in your mind, emotions and body, the easier the transformation process will be.

Each cell of your body carries within itself a magnificent part of the God-Essence. And as this new energy field caresses your cellular structure, it frees the essence that lies within. So when you are seated in meditation, it would help to direct the cells to relax and to release outmoded beliefs and stale emotions, relax and release repetitious thoughts and bodily tensions. As cellular relaxation takes place, there is a sense in the being of letting go. It is this relaxation, this trusting of the energy, that brings a deep and continuous feeling of the trustworthiness of God-Consciousness.

Miracles

One of the greatest sorrows for those of us who work with the earth plane comes from the sense that very few people today deeply believe in the power of miracles.[1] You are very willing to acknowledge miracles of the past, such as those surrounding Jesus, Buddha or St. Francis, but there is tremendous doubt and a deep belief that miracles are not possible for you.

To remind you that miracles are not just something which happened long ago, we will update some of these miraculous events. You are all aware that St. Francis of Assisi received the marks of the stigmata upon his body. The stigmata are the four points of the nails and the slash on the side of the body of Christ on the cross. As a final act of Francis' complete love and desire to identify fully with his Lord, the Seraphim came from the unseen world, enveloped Francis in Its wings, and the stigmata were placed upon him. That was a long time ago, so it's easy to think it has nothing to do with you today.

But let's move to the similar experience of a very devout Italian priest who lived in the earlier part of this century. His name was Padre Pio and, through his love for Christ, he also received the stigmata. The difficulty he faced because of the Catholic Church's obvious reluctance to acknowledge this kind of miraculous happening was extensive. But proof of the miracle worker comes from the miraculous results of that person's being on the earth plane. The stories of Padre Pio reflect miracles. He bandaged his bleeding wounds, and when people learned he had the stigmata, they began using the bandages for healing, and cures happened. Through those happenings, he was able to re-awaken people to the knowledge that miracles were possible.

In this day and age, the miraculous is still available to those who yearn for the Divine with all their heart and soul. By your very love and desire to find the God within, you create a feeling, a power which then goes out into the world and touches people's hearts and minds. It's the energy generated from your search for God that sets up a hope in others and deeply touches people who have no knowledge of you or what you are doing.

Just as Padre Pio sought and found the Lord within, and carried an outer statement of that experience in the form of the stigmata, so did his finding send waves of light, power and wonder not only into the Catholic world, but beyond it. At the end of his life, when he was again allowed by the church to hold audience, people came from all over the world to be blessed by him. There were Hindus, Buddhists, Catholics, non-believers, Muslims, all kinds of seekers, and they came away with a sense that it must be possible for the rest of mankind to have the same experiences. Padre Pio serves as a reminder that turning your awareness toward a single-pointed, enlightened consciousness such as the Christ, and asking for that great enlightened awareness to illumine you, will result in miracles.

You do not have to walk this journey alone, my friends. There is help available from all the great, wise ones who have come before you. Their light, their awakening, is still present to be received by you as a gift. Beings such as the Christ or the Buddha, having manifested vast, enlightened awareness for the benefit of the planet, leave behind very strong energy fields for you to participate in. These days the names may have changed but the energy remains the same.

Refreshment for one who is heavy laden comes when you wash away the belief that your burdens are real and replace them with the awareness that you are something far vaster, far deeper and far wiser. Please remember that each person who has turned toward any wise one and found rapport and enlightenment with them has added to the power and beauty of the energy field they sought. It is easy to see how you benefit, since in the ensuing years thousands of people have come into conscious awareness, thus adding to the availability of those great ones. By relentlessly pursuing the desire for union with these energies, it can be done. And when it is, the rewards are beyond explanation. No earth plane words can reflect the glory, the safety, the awe and the boundless gratitude one feels when this deep connection has been made.

Goddesses

I have been asked to discuss goddess energy and the maximum way to blend with, understand, and bring this energy to light. You must realize as you begin to work with material about the ancient goddesses, you are working with ideas from old civilizations and even some that have been entirely forgotten. The image of the goddess is deeply buried in the unconscious of the planet. For every so-called male power available, there is a so-called feminine power as well. One of the definite movements of the 'New Age' is a re-emergence back into people's awareness of the 'forgotten powers' of goddess energies.

It has been a long time since the goddess has been taken

seriously. The motion of the planet has been toward the masculine development of consciousness rather than the feminine. Today, there is the necessity of balancing the masculine and feminine, therefore we must have a way to re-approach this very heavily masculine hierarchy of religion. It is time for new revelations about all of the goddess powers and it is time for both men and women to take an inward approach toward any of the goddess energy they feel drawn to. New awareness will awaken inspiration and a sense of what new wisdom the ancient ones have to offer.

These goddess energies have been growing in awareness as the planet has changed. Nothing stays the same. Just as Christ-Consciousness has expanded over the years, so have these feminine energies. And the new goddess has something new to say, something much more in alignment with this day and age and what needs to be done now. The feminine is doing its best to permeate this entire planet with its ability to harmonize the masculine and the feminine. All of the vast energy fields realize the time of union is upon us. To bring this about, all separations must be removed. There is no reality in the mental sense of separation, the emotional feeling of separation, or the physical 'reality' of separation. There is only One, so the new goddess energy will bring opportunities of discovering how best to create harmony on all levels of being, for the male as well as the female. It can teach how to use feminine power to permeate the structures of the masculine with gentleness and wisdom, so both can participate in the dance of life with wholeness, not as separated consciousness.

Was this turning away from the goddess energy, many centuries ago, some kind of mistake? Of course not. The feminine energy then was strong and it was as if the masculine had to turn away from the goddess wisdom in order to initiate the search for its own understanding. The masculine is now firmly manifest with dynamic power, and some would say has perhaps overextended itself. Whatever the case, a new blending is now appropriate, for the feminine energy needs to come forward again in a more refined way than was possible many centuries ago when the human psyche was just beginning to understand itself.

As we observe this co-mingling of humankind, we look forward to all differences being seen as balancing, corresponding, blending aspects, not as contradictory. We look forward to the masculine feeling its own safety and ease, because in safety it will relax. The masculine has to learn to let go. It has to be shaken up so new openings within the psyche of the ruling masculine belief structures can take place. Then the feminine energy can move gently into the existing structures, and instead of destroying them, make its influence known in a nurturing way. You need not destroy the masculine to feel the impact of the feminine.

In many places on the planet, there is a preoccupation with earthquakes, which are simply a shaking up and changing of physical earth forms. These are places where new life enters, where new lifestyles begin, where new ways of relating to each other and to ideas take shape. These are places where new forms can come into being. Much shaking up is necessary for the feminine to permeate the openings as they present themselves. So, please bear this in mind when you hear about predictions of great earth changes. They may have nothing to do with the earth itself, but are rather required for this exciting blending, at long last, of the masculine and feminine upon it.

For those of you who are concerned about healing this planet, goddess energy can present much useful information. Any of you who have spent quiet time in relationship with the earth must realize it is feminine. As you look at its hills, its valleys and flowing streams, you sense a deep feminine aspect in the land. As you feel the surge of the oceans and the movements of the tide, again one senses the feminine. Being a feminine planet, it is therefore logical it would be the domain of the goddess and she would desire to help restore the balance so badly needed here. She is willing, indeed anxious, to bestow on anyone who will attune and listen, the lessons, guidance and inspiration necessary for the harmony of the physical planet to take place.

There is a simplicity and deep power in the silence of the heart of nature. You would do well to approach the goddess through the natural world. She moves with greater ease in the mountains, valleys and oceans, than she does in the regimented concrete of the masculine world. As you stand in nature, look at the mountains and ask that all of these magnificent points of power be used to inspire you. As you feel the vastness of the sea, ask for that hidden power deep within to fill you with enlightened knowing. Wherever you live, look at the sky. The goddess is present there as well. If you cannot move out of your home, surround yourself with reflections of her natural beauty, of the nature of things. She can be found with ease in a flowering plant, in the sun on a window sill, in the midst of a ghetto, if she is approached with the same open reverence you would use if you were in the midst of a field of sunflowers. She comes to anyone who is willing to approach her with humility, devotion, and the desire to be inspired in her name.

So how then does all of this affect you? What is the goddess energy calling on you to do? It is basically asking you to look at your own way of relating to belief structures that are not your own. It is giving you all encouragement to seek ways, with gentle, nurturing awareness, to move harmlessly in your relationships, not only with other people, but with all other awarenesses that inhabit this earth plane. This includes the very basic earth upon which you stand. It is asking for a movement of the feminine, an energy that penetrates with love, understanding and a peaceful heart. It is only when mutual coming together is experienced that real delight is shared and felt.

The goddess knows destruction does not bring mutual pleasure. Her energy is asking for a new way of being, a gentle, yet empowered persistence that wears away the old belief structures.

I am not speaking to just the feminine. I am speaking to each of you, because each of you contains that deep, penetrating, gentle, all-accepting feminine consciousness. That which is the receptor, that which takes in all things, that which has a heart big enough to hold the universe, is what I am talking about. That is the new state of being.

What I am asking for is an approach to the goddess with a consciousness unfettered by the past, unfettered by myth or story. Approach her with an open heart, asking for a direct, intimate and enlightening connection. Ask that she guide you, not only in your daily life, but with her wisdom, to approach the God which she also represents. It's time for new truth, new inspiration, new revelation, and in this realm, miracles are also possible.

---

[1] *A miracle is an uplifting and revelatory experience of a Divine nature.*

BREATHE IN, BREATHE OUT

June 4, 1988
Tres Piedras, New Mexico

I was recently asked to explain why medita-tion is valuable. Meditation, done properly in whatever form it takes, has as its basic function *the conscious absorption of life force into your body* so you can have access to more power, more energy and more awareness. This 'life force' does not tell you what to do with the energy once it's in you. You can rob a bank or you can find God. It's entirely up to you.

Meditation is a state where you are constantly recharging the Light within, which gives you the power to do anything you want. Your 'free will' operates through the choices you make around what you want to do with this power. If you decide to find God, you will discover ways to be continuously attuned to that inner decision in the midst of whatever is going on in your life. You will discover ways to use the power your meditation has generated to experience what you long to experience. You will use the power of awareness to carry you again and again to the point of inner Light that is God.

As your focused awareness grows stronger, you will discover you deeply want to be in alignment with what you would call God's will. Meditation helps you to know what that is. In medita-tion you take in the breath and let out the breath. You have awareness that watches it come in, and watches it go out. You pay attention. You slow down. You become aware you are asking to *experience what is within you.*

A basic truth will be obvious if you do the following: Take a deep breath and *hold it.* Hold it! Hold it! The obvious truth is: *You cannot survive on the inbreath alone.* You cannot move, function and be alive in the physical body when you only take breath in. The delightful job of those in a physical body is to learn the technique of living with inbreath and outbreath, to understand what they mean, to know the difference between them, and to fill yourself constantly with them.

When you decide to become 'spiritual,' most of you start by taking inbreaths, and you breathe in and breathe in and breathe in and all of a sudden you are unconscious because you have been breathing in too long! Inbreath is taking in, receiving, being filled from the outside. This can take the form of such things as reading books, going to lectures and workshops, finding a guru or teacher, or even traveling to India to find God. Outbreath happens when you extend from within yourself out into your world. This can take the form of working for a hospice, doing selfless service, joining a peace walk, or just putting all you have learned on inbreath into practice moment after moment.

You have set up what I see as a great paradox. On the one hand, you are told to surrender to God's will—that's an inbreath. On the other hand, you have been told you create your own reality and you are responsible for it—that's an outbreath. Why aren't you in total chaos over those polarities? How can you have your will taken over and live from the center of God-Awareness and God-Love and at the same time create your own reality? Unless you address this dilemma on a deep level of your being, you will continue to be confused by this paradox.

So, what do inbreath and surrender mean? Inbreath is the receiving of vaster energies and the *surrender to that feeling.* No action, no thought, just feeling. But to be able to take a deep, clear inbreath of God, you must first remove any obstacles that stand in the way. These obstacles are the things you believe you must eliminate or acquire before you are ready to feel the presence of God. Find out what your inner rules are. What do you believe you must develop or get rid of on the inner planes before you can find God? For example: "I will never find God if I do not learn how to meditate deeply," or "I can only experience God if I have a loving heart." Then, what are your rules for living out in the world? "If I don't treat people nicely, God will never love me." "If I have money, I can't have God." The first movement toward balanced breathing is to get in touch with the particular standards you must meet in order to find what you want. Examine your particular set of beliefs, because those beliefs *will* keep you from surrendering to the God experience. Face them and they will begin to loosen their hold on you.

Now, what of outbreath and creating your own reality? Your outbreath creates something every moment. For the most part, you have been creating out of your unconscious, a part of the psyche that contains patterns of your past. But creating out of the past makes the future *like* the past. To stop this pattern, you must find a way to stop using the unconscious as the creator of your future. You must be willing to take the risk of being a conscious creator, *not* from your unconscious, but consciously with God. You must be willing to be a Co-Creator. A Co-Creator is one who decides what attributes of God-Self they want to experience and then concentrates on those attributes until they appear. For example, do you want peace? Joy? A deep knowing of who you are? The light of consciousness? Then keep remembering those are the things you want, and when you go within, expect to find them! Since these are attributes found both within you and God, you can co-create their manifestation in your life.

Creating A State of Inner Awareness

Please take out paper and pencil. We will begin with an exercise to illustrate creating through the outbreath. On a large piece of paper, draw a circular shape that touches all four sides. This will create a space that appears either as a circle or an egg-shape.

*The challenge is to dare and fill that shape with things which will make you happy. Again and again you define your lives, not in positive terms about who you **do** want to be, but in negative terms of who you **do not** want to be. As long as this is your orientation, you will be fighting the natural flow of the universe. The universe wants to help you create those things that give you happiness. The universe moves toward joy and light and creative abundance. You see this in the incredible abundance of nature. It creates endless delights out of itself. The same is possible for you. So begin by deciding what abundance you really want, and what creative delights you really want to experience. Then list those delights carefully in the circle on your paper. Be as specific as you can because you are beginning to create a new sense of who you are.*

Pause. Exercise continues.

*Holding these creative hopes in mind, we are now going to influence the future. Imagine it's your last day on earth and you are quietly dying. Picture yourself in a relaxed position on a comfortable seat next to a flowing river. Take as long as you need to really **feel** and **see** this clearly. When you feel some degree of reality about this image, ask yourself what specific energies you want to be filled with when you leave this realm of existence. Don't just limit it to those things of the so-called spirit. Address the fact you have a physical body. What condition do you want it to be in? You have a mind. What thoughts do you want present? You have emotions. What emotions do you want to feel? What do you want your inner self to be like? Address the totality of your being. If someone were to walk up to you as you were dying, what would you want them to see and feel? What would you want **them** to experience as they sit quietly with you? When this scenario has been **deeply felt**, write down those things you found you wished to be at the end of your life. Place these in the sphere on your paper.*

Pause. Exercise continues.

So far in this vision you have been seated. Now stand up and begin a walk. Where you walk is up to you. It can be beside the river, or upon a mountain, along the beach, in a meadow, through a shopping mall, or wherever your particular idea of walking at this ending time would be. As you are walking, look at what you pass and record everything you experience, as you notice now one thing, then another. What is your **response** *to all that you see? What do you,* **now filled with your chosen energies,** *feel as you move from flower to tree to bush? Describe these energies fully on your paper.*

Now that you have experienced the effect you have on your world, let us experience how your world would respond to you. You go by a bush, stop a moment. How does the bush respond? The tree? The flower? The animals? The stop sign on the corner? What do these things see **in you?** *As you move along, get a feeling for how those things in your world would perceive you as you walk through them. How would your world respond if you were filled with this kind of intense, aware presence? Please take in everything. If you happen to be by a stream, include the fish and rocks. Make this* **real.** *Envision the impact you would have on the environment if you were simply walking about in this new, expanded state of Wholeness.*

Pause until finished.

As you begin to create the vision of how this action of outbreath would affect your world, you also create the chance of really having it manifest. That which you dwell upon becomes real. The more you remember what you want to experience and give to the world, the more you *will* experience those energies. Please understand, *you are afraid of creating your own life or death because you are afraid of creating against God.* But, if you really are a son or daughter of God, it is time for you to claim the fullness of what that means. The Divine does not want the worst for you or even the mediocre. It wants the *best.*

As you imagine yourself experiencing all the highest attributes you can imagine, you are fulfilling God's will for you. Peace. Wisdom. Strength. Power. Limitlessness. Love. This is a beginning. What you have written down is the beginning of what you can do, and what you can have in your life, if you start being courageous and stop being afraid of creation. The view of yourself you have placed within the egg-shaped space is the possible you. It isn't by chance you created the particular image you see there. You have the total potential to be that now, not in the future, but right now! *If you can imagine it, you can become it.* It is *already* you, in there, in that egg, waiting to be born. How do you make it manifest? Concentrate on it. Experience what those energies *feel* like. How many times have we said energy follows thought? What you turn your awareness to becomes manifest. The job is simply to make it more and more real.

The 'trick' of creation on the physical plane is simple. 'Above' this plane is another world we could call the world of the geometric perfection. When you imagine, you are activating this geometric world with your mind and will. When you have put enough power into your vision by concentrating on it, it projects 'downward' from the geometric world into this one. The world of geometric perfection does not have moral judgment. It is a power source. Just as you can use electricity to either illuminate a lamp or to execute someone, so does this power have nothing to say about what is created from it. It is just there to be used. It supplies you with abundant power to be used as you 'will.'

So the view of yourself you created today is now somewhere in that geometric world, taking form to the extent that you empower it. The more you return your awareness to it, the more you activate the principle of that plane of existence. You do not need to know *how* it is going to manifest in your lives, my friends. If you start to worry about the 'how' you are lost because you will once again be caught up in limitations of earth plane consciousness. *Every* time you have a thought, it activates a pattern *somewhere*. So choose what you want to activate.

Choosing A State of Consciousness

Each of you possess what we will call various 'bodies'—the mental, emotional and physical, among them. Those bodies can be activated by both 'lower' and 'higher' vibrations. Everyone is familiar with the lower vibrational patterns of the mind. They include judgment, self-righteousness, self-pity and projection, among many others. But think about the wonder of the mind. What would your life be like if you didn't have the ability to use it to learn about things you wanted to know? What if you couldn't grapple with the abstract, or experience such mental delights as inspiration and creative understanding? Think what your world would be like if the higher vibrations of the mind were not present.

And what of the emotional body? Emotions which run at a low vibration are often full of tedious, unfolding dramas that engage you and demand other people's attention. Emotional drama filled with anger, resentment, fear and accusation is like a blinding storm which engulfs everyone so they can no longer see what is present. But there is nothing more amazing than the high vibrational emotions such as wonder, love, awe or creative passion, and there is a part of you that knows it.

Then let's talk about the body. There is no question that there is a lower octave to the body. Man's inhumanity to man is one of the greatest horrors of the planet. What one human body inflicts on another can be seen as the most painful of earth plane experiences. No one denies that. But do not take the position of blaming the body for everything, thereby losing the joy and delight of the higher vibrations of the physical. What would your life be like if you couldn't see, smell, taste and hear? What would it be like trapped in the body, unable to touch and feel those things outside it? The physical body is where you interface with this planet most directly and also where the joys of the mental and emotional bodies are experienced.

There are many states of consciousness. I am asking you to dare to risk, to imagine and to envision the highest of these you really wish to experience. The best of you is in that sphere on your paper—*the very best*. If you want to talk in terms of giving to the

Divine, lift the very best of yourself up to this unseen realm of creation and say, *"This is what I want! This is who I want to be!"* Recharge that image day after day, remembering, feeling, touching, tasting what you want. This is the best you know for yourself at this moment and this is what you are asking of the Divine. "Let's be this one, God, let's do it." And the Divine says, "You bet!" And in that moment you both begin to create it.

The greatest barrier to using this method of creating in your life is your belief that it's an *imaginary* journey, that it somehow isn't real. This is not true. Imaginings are the stuff out of which you create your world. You imagine it first and then it manifests. It is not the other way around. To the extent you imagine boldly, deeply and vastly in your own life, that is the extent to which you will begin to experience the vast, bold power of creativity.

Sponge Consciousness

To illustrate this point, let's use an analogy of you as a sponge. I use the image of a dried-up sponge to present a painfully contracted, fearful human, which sometimes you are. Fear gives you the feeling you do not have the ability to stretch, expand and move. You feel you are not free, but are always bound by rules, controlled and always trying, never Being. You are afraid to create change because you are afraid you will 'do it wrong.' But there comes a moment when you take a chance. You fall in love and find yourself expanding, lighter, more inspired. Then when the love is no longer working, you find yourself contracting. You get a good job, you expand. You get fired, you contract. It doesn't even have to be something big. You're feeling great one day. You go out in the world and someone says, "What are you smiling about?" and you are deflated. So the horizontal, linear part of your life goes up and down, expanding and contracting. But I would like to suggest you take yourself, as sponge, and immerse yourself in an ocean of God-Awareness. This immersing will expand you, and open you up.

You have only to look at your life to see those dead areas you have created out of fear or pain. There is no *blame* attached to this. Because you were not aware you could consciously create for expansion, you created in another way. You created without *conscious* choice and became trapped in your own creations. The way out is through conscious, creative choice, which we are going to undertake now.

Let us try a ritual to explain this. Remember, transformation begins with imagination. With the image of 'spongeness,' go outside and find something which represents that state of 'spongeness,' something which can expand and contract. Bring this object back. We will act out the immersion of the sponge into God-Awareness in a ritualistic form. Why do we use ritual? Because ritual impresses the 'unconscious' parts of you. Things get serious very fast when you set about to perform a ritual, either by yourself or with a like-minded group.

Pause.

The object you have selected stands as representative of the dried up, contorted, fearful part of your consciousness. Since that is also a part of you at this moment, you cannot just throw it away. Nor can you take it and put it in the garbage and have somebody else come along and take care of it. You created this fearful part of your experience with the same amount of hope and passion you have created everything else. You created it because you felt you needed to. It represents an incredible amount of effort, risk, and hope, along with much tears and laughter. Please look upon it with all due reverence and gratitude. Don't look to destroy it. That which you wish to change, you transform, not destroy. Nothing needs to be destroyed or annihilated. But many things can be transformed by the power of your awareness. You can consciously activate that part of your psyche which is the transformer by turning your awareness inward and *feeling* the place within you which contains the *power* to envision and transform. Don't allow yourself to doubt this energy is present within you—just go in and *feel* it!

Transformation Ritual

*Form a circle if you are in a group, and place in the center a bowl of water large enough to hold all the objects collected. Remembering it is time to take that fearful part of you as represented by whatever you are holding, drop it into the vast expanse of Divine Wholeness as represented by the water. As the water permeates the object and it begins to expand, be totally conscious of releasing and expanding. Tell yourself it is time to transform those outmoded parts into the new attributes you have chosen for yourself. Make the statement to yourself that the greater choice is to leave all useless energies behind and move into a vaster realm. Let that be the intention. Sit in a quiet spot and notice the difference in the object expanded in the water, and try to feel that expansion in you as well. Spend time allowing yourself to really **imagine**, visualizing clearly your life and yourself with these 'new' choices alive in you. Stay with this new feeling until you really feel something happen. This is **real**—this is transformation at work—and it **does** work.*

Pause until completed.

Creating With Integrity

We have been working with the concept that out of the geometric perfection comes the power to help you manifest your choices. It must have occurred to you there may be hidden dangers that accompany this process. So what assurance do you have that when you begin to consciously use this power, you will not also be creating 'monsters' that will be unleashed on the earth plane and on you? To explain this, I will give you a basic example of what truly happens in the world of creativity.

Let us use as an example one of the greatest villains in your perception, Adolf Hitler. He begins with a vision to free the people of his land from what seem to him to be overwhelming social and economic problems. As he envisions his goals, the form takes shape in the realm of the geometric perfection. His desire becomes so large it takes an incredible amount of power to feed it. He would not have been able to manifest a dream of such proportions, affecting so many others and so much of the world, if thousands upon thousands of people had not filled in the form with him. Adolph Hitler alone, would have tried to manipulate the world, and he would have failed. He simply did not have sufficient power to make such an immense dream manifest by himself. It had to be filled in and made larger by the great numbers of people who heard the dream and also desired its manifestation. Anywhere along the line of his creation, the people could have said, "No, this is not for me," and it would have ended. But they didn't.

What does this say about you? When you create something you feel has integrity and usefulness in it, I do not think you could fool yourself or your friends for very long if it was not for the good of those concerned. Creating from love with an open heart feels differently than creating out of revenge, anger or separateness. So be discriminating as you create choices of action in your world. If you have any doubts about your desire manifesting the best for everyone, state your willingness to have it left unmanifested if it is not of the highest. This is a safeguard you can rely upon with confidence. Trust yourself. Do you really think Hitler felt uplifted by his actions, or did he feel driven? You know the difference between feeling driven and feeling uplifted and whole. As you progress, you will learn to trust this process. You *do* know how to create the good, the true and the beautiful in your life, and you will grow in confidence as you see and feel that it is working.

Creating Karma

Someone asked me what to do with the doubts which arise when you allow yourself to create what you want. They believe your 'karma' creates for you, in spite of you—and you have no control over the process. So, how does karma fit in to creating?

A *linear* concept of karma as cause and effect is valuable for a certain state in your unfoldment. At one stage, it helps to believe you reap what you sow. Also, ritualistic commitment—a belief in the absolute truth of the rules of religion, is found in every culture of the world. It's a way of moving safely toward experiencing your connection with the Divine. When you follow these rules, you feel a sense of safety, and this approach works beautifully for many people. But comes the day when the rules are not enough. You long to experience a more direct communion with God. Before you move on, we ask that you express gratitude for what you may have received. You gave a lot and received a lot from any path followed with honor and integrity. It is a wonderful journey, my friends. But finally one has to know for oneself what the Divine really is.

Those of you who are familiar with my work know I have a very different concept of karma than is held in most belief structures. Karma, as generally expressed, is a limited description of what is, in reality, an expansive truth. The concept of karma, as I view it, is a set of magnificent explosions, which start when you burst through the birthing experience into what you call life on the earth plane. You are like the dandelion, yellow-faced one moment, and in the next a white sphere of individuated seedpods, separate, yet still together. Then a breath of wind comes and 'poof,' each pod begins its journey. They move off in all directions as the wind takes them up. Some float, some fall, but that 'poof' is the moment I'm talking about. It is an explosion. It is not linear, it is an explosion! This is how I see your beginnings and your journey.

The 'explosion' is the beginning of the delightful experiment you have chosen to undergo here on planet earth. You not only feel and live your own life as you walk your path, but you feel from all around you the sound and motion of all your fellow humans and everything of the whole planetary makeup. You have no idea how much you affect each other, not just other people, but the entire planet as well. It is not difficult to experience. If you want to try it, just go to a hospital and sit there. Then go to a church or temple and sit there, and then, try something different—go to a football game or a quiet place in nature. You will feel the subtle effects each place has upon you, and the effect you have upon each other.

As you explode, you bump into each other. It sometimes seems like a very light bump, but in fact, a lot of energy flows from one person to another. The *delight* of that movement is when you dance together. The *pain* of it is when you bruise each other. But don't worry, it's nothing very long-lasting. Take two aspirins and call God in the morning.

Karma can be felt like the breeze you feel on a warm summer day. It has the effect of pushing you in a particular direction. It is like a stream of power that guides you, moves you and urges you toward one choice, then another. It cannot *make* you choose. You understand things when you are 'in the now.' When you are awake in the present, you can see the reality of what's happening without fooling yourself in the slightest. After all, whatever predicament you are in, you created it. That you know. However the situation looks to you karmically, whatever you have or haven't done in the past is not significant. In the moment, you have the energy to move things in a different direction.

You know what your ego feels like when it is in action. If you don't, just take a moment to experience the feelings when you dwell on judgment of someone or indulge in self-pity or anger. Then still yourself and consciously call in a higher order of energy. Ego energy moves horizontally. Divine energy moves vertically. So you, moving along a horizontal path, are now calling in the vertical Divine movement. You are calling in and blending with God. In that moment, you will feel a 'quickening' or movement within, as though something deep and full is moving in you.

So, keep remembering the things you truly want to manifest, and then allow the Divine to help you create them. Try this experiment for the next six or eight months. Remember what you want to create, then select what is *most* important to you. Of all the possible things, there is one that really delights you, fills you, and is in alignment with your highest goal. Focus on that one. When the doubts come in, ask yourself if your life isn't fuller acting as if there were a God for you to blend with. *Knowing* if your life pattern is going to fulfill itself may not be *conscious* knowledge at this moment. But what have you got to lose by continuing to feel the dream? Allow the wonder, beauty, mystery and majesty of the Divine to fill out the dream, and let life manifest that which it can for you.

Divine energy is moving all over the planet. And in the end the greatest gift you will have given yourself is the blending with God, with that Energy. Please use it for your own bounteous delight. You are constantly creating your life. So do it consciously on your own behalf, out of the abundance of your Being. Don't be afraid. When you live a linear life, you may think you know what "the good life" is. My friends, as good as your life is, it's not the "good life" because it's missing what makes life totally, magically, abundantly wondrous. It's missing the feeling of being consciously blended with the Divine. And how will you find this feeling? *By daring!* Daring to look past a world full of tedium, of sameness. That creative substance which is Life will fill out any form you hold in your mind. So hold the highest. Of yourself you can do nothing, but without you it cannot be done.

There is but One Self, my friends, One Self and *and you are It.*

STRENGTH
IN THE FACE OF ADVERSITY

April 15, 1989
Taos, New Mexico

All of you have moments when you allow yourself to feel fear rising within you. It may come as a result of an event during your waking day, or in the loneliness of night. So, how do you face this? Begin by allowing yourself to name these fears. Bring them into sharp focus in your conscious mind. When you begin to name them, a curious fact arises. You will find most of them have to do with the fact you have a body, and you are afraid that you are *powerless* to change what happens to that body. You believe in your own powerlessness.

To help you shake this belief, I would like to put you in touch with an energy field many of you have refused to accept—that of *strength*. You are convinced you could not possibly be strong or have strength, yet if you could believe this about yourself, you would be able to face your worst fears. The attribute of strength can make maximum use of your pain or help you to integrate with the beauty and wonder of life. Your fear comes because you are afraid some physical, mental or emotional anguish will come upon you that will overwhelm you. But when you access your *inner strength,* you will have the help you need to face any adversity with peace and power.

My friends, I want to make it very clear that strength and

God are the same. God is all-powerful. It is omniscient, omni-present, magnificently bliss-filled, and consciously aware. Strength is a gift from God that provides you with the necessary courage to find out who you are no matter what is happening. By yourself you can do nothing, but this inner strength, which has always been a part of you, can be called upon in an instant. It is an existing, clear, decisive energy field which is always available, so we shall spend some time contacting this strength within.

In ancient and modern myths, the hero is rarely an ineffec-tual person who sits on the sidelines of life. Heroes and heroines demonstrate the ability to take decisive and courageous action, which is also what you want to do. You are on a heroic journey this very moment. Your heroic journey is constantly unfolding. You are here in the world not just to sit, but to act, and to act from a place of power that will result in positive changes in your world.

You are here to feel life, to feel life without fear and to be alive with the delight of life. What stands between you and that feeling is the fear you cannot be victorious, that somehow you will fail. Every one of you has, to some degree, the deep fear of being a failure. Experiencing your own inner strength is a way to ensure that you can be heroic, that whatever happens, *you* will have control over your life.

When you look to the external world for strength, you become weakened. When you rely on the strength within, you become strong. Strength does not come from 'out there.' Love does not come from 'out there.' Deep knowing does not come from 'out there.' You are looking in the wrong place, and in looking at those things which rise and fall, come and go, please and displease, you miss the real. You miss that which never changes, which is ever-reliable. What you are looking for is a consistent feeling of strength which never leaves you. I am not saying this gives you a total awareness of God-Consciousness. But I do say, if you keep falling back into feeling strength, it will help deepen your inner life until you touch upon your own pure, conscious awareness. This sense of strength will guide you past the layers of worldly confusion to the Deep Self. So we simply present as many things as possible to help you remember this.

Stop a moment, close your eyes and allow yourself to feel strength. Do not think about strength or picture yourself as strong. Simply be still and ask to feel strength. It is there. You can feel it.

Short pause.

As you become more aware of this strength, you will come to know that it is also love, also peace, also light. The closer and more familiar with strength you become, the less you will mind if things in your world are not exactly to your liking. You will not mind adversity as much because a sense of your power over it will be growing. Instead of trying to push away frightening experiences, you will pull difficult things closer to you, simply to give yourself the chance to feel your own strength. You will respond to difficulties with heroic courage. You will stop playing the victim. You will sense that nothing outside yourself can inundate you. Whatever happens, strength remains, and this knowledge will give you peace.

If you do not know you are strong, you will not be at peace. If you do not know you are strong, you will not allow yourself to relax enough to find out who you are. Relaxation comes from assurance. When relaxation is present, you begin to feel the attributes within that have always been there. The attributes you assign to those who have become God-Realized, such as peace, love, joy, spontaneous motion, arise from this energy field of inner strength. You maximize the feeling of this particular energy field by becoming fearless. So let us discuss fearlessness.

When you descend beneath the surface of consciousness, you often move into what you would call the shadows, the dark places where fear lurks. When you find yourself in those darker areas of consciousness, the first suggestion is, do not pretend they are not real, that they are not there. Do not run. For example, in a dream, you are running amuck and killing people. Do not awaken and pretend it has nothing to do with you. Until you allow yourself to understand there is a part of you capable of running amuck, you will never resolve your fears. You will remain powerless. You must stop running from your dark thoughts and wishes, and just allow them to surface. When they are seen for what they are, they will reveal themselves to be what makes you a part of humankind. All humans have such potential, harmful possibilities lurking within. That is what feeling totally human means. To *know* they are within you makes you powerful, not helpless. To admit you are human with human frailties, gives you the opportunity to hold those thoughts and possibilities quietly within you, and then to perform the miracle. The miracle is to simply accept they are present, and ask to feel the strength which gives you the power not to act on those thoughts or feelings. You call on that inner strength to gently dilute them, to soften the hardness of those images, and to leave you stronger for the attempt. You ask to feel what *else* is present besides those feelings. Yes, they are there. But what else is there? Sit quietly and ask to feel the attributes of your God-Self. Ask to feel the peace, the light, the God within.

Let's use an imaginary presentation to show how fears attack you. Picture a hollow space within your body in which all your fears are collected. They are held in by a top which is very loosely hinged. When the top opens, some of the fears slip out to arise in your mind. This happens mostly in the night, during sleep, when you have taken your hands off the controls. When nighttime relaxation takes place, the lid falls open and some of the fears escape. Even when you have dreams you don't recall, you can wake up fearful, or you can simply be sitting quietly, doing nothing, when suddenly something triggers off a fear response. It can be something you see, or something you hear, or just being relaxed. Since relaxation is necessary for experiencing God, you need to learn what to do with the fears so they become a smaller part of your life, not the whole of it.

Take some time now to move your awareness to that part of you where your fears exist, sit quietly and allow them to come up. As they arise, identify them. You do not need to resolve them because in reality there is no problem. These fears are based on a false view of yourself. They are based on the idea that all you are is a vulnerable human being in a body. They are based on the idea you are somehow small and alone, isolated, and under the control of very capricious energy fields, none of which is true. You are not a body and you are not subject to the laws the body presents to you. Your happiness and safety do not lie with your body or anyone else's. As long as you identify with body, these fears will continue to run your life, keeping you from the spontaneous enjoyment of living. Unfaced fears keep you from the delight of living. So allow them to surface, and face them gently and non-judgmentally. Allow them to move up into your consciousness.

A helpful way to assist this process is to write all of your fears down. Take them to the worst extremity you can. Make sure you look at all the parts of your life, such as health, family, money, sanity, business, death, all of it. Your environment is constantly bombarding you with fears and it is time to look at them. Take all the time you need. If today's work is not enough, do it day after day until you feel comfortable with each one. Gently feel their presence within you.

Pause.

Now turn your awareness to what else is present. Then ask yourself if you are willing to feel strength.

Pause until completed.

You might say it's obvious you would be willing to be strong, but it may not be so. Part of you has been trained to feel you need to be taken care of, and if you are strong, perhaps no one will take care of you. Strength might mean loneliness. Also, there have been times when you have felt victimized and ineffectual in the world. You will have to be willing to drop all such remembrances of the past and forgive all the people and events that you saw as conspiring to make you a 'poor little thing.' You will have to let all that go because you cannot be strong and weak at the same time.

Strength is an energy, and when it is present, weakness is not experienced. So you must choose.

You are either strong, capable, expansive, delightfully alive in this moment, or you are not. If you are not ready to be strong inside, you will always find something outside yourself to blame for your weakness. Right now, you have to drop the view of yourself which has created your world so other people will take care of you. Someone who is strong does not need to be "taken care" of. Someone who is strong has the inner capacity to let anything happen. When they do, those around them are released from the obligation of treating them in any certain way.

When you begin to act out of strength, your world changes because you are no longer trying to manipulate it. Since all events can produce strength, you cease to manipulate your life and others in order to have specific events arise. *Any* event will do. When you move from the external 'drama' and go inside and begin to feel your own strength, you will stimulate strength in those around you. Strength in you brings out strength in others. Internal strength, when you are concentrating on it, is one of the greatest powers in the physical body. Whatever difficulty arises, go to that strength. There is a sense of being empowered, which empowers others.

Many of you are afraid that someone, something or some group can gain power over you, forcing you to do things you don't really want to do. As best you can, you set up your lives so no one has this power over you. "Getting in touch with your own power" is currently an important psychological technique designed to help people move away from these fears. People who utilize this technique tend to move, initially, from the role of victim to victimizer. All they have done is to exchange positions, and in the end find that unsatisfactory as well. But this does not last for long. They will learn that by going within and resting in that strength, which you have just done, whatever happens 'out there' becomes acceptable, and then they relax into allowing things to be as they are.

It is frightening to let your life do whatever it will. It's terrifying to think what might happen to you if things don't go the way you want. But that is what I am asking you to face. Release the desire to have anything outside yourself appear in any certain way, and simply concentrate on the feeling of strength within. In the midst of the most difficult dialogue, instead of paying attention to the dialogue, drop down deeply into yourself, feel your strength and keep quiet. See how it feels and see what happens.

Let's talk about how strength in the material world can help. Let us say you owe a lot of money, or are not physically in the state of health you wish to be, or perhaps your emotions are not as stable as you would desire. You must first understand, the problem is not what you think it is, and you are not really upset about what you think you are. The problem is not in your state of money or health or emotions. The problem is the feeling of *helplessness* you experience in the face of these events. Helplessness is the problem. If you did not feel helpless over a physical disability, it would not be difficult. If you did not feel helpless without money, it would not be a problem. If you did not feel helpless in the midst of emotional storms, they would not be so upsetting. And when you do get through one so-called problem, you know there is always another waiting to be dealt with. What will it be? Are you afraid of losing your great love affair? Look again, more closely this time. Perhaps you are afraid of the helpless feeling you get when you have no one to love you, and no one to love. In the end, you are not upset by your lover leaving, you are afraid love will no longer be in your heart, and *you* will no longer feel the presence of love. You must touch on the real fear, which is the helplessness you feel.

Strength Is Awareness

The concept of creating your own reality is a popular topic of discussion. At one level of your development, it is absolutely essential you understand that thoughts create, and what you hold in your mind is what manifests in your world. This is called creating your own reality. It's nothing very fancy, just that which you concentrate upon manifests. But on the very deepest level it does not matter what you create, because today it will be this way, tomorrow a different way, and in the next lifetime you will turn it all upside down and it will be totally different again. Nothing *you* create stays as you created it. It is always changing into something else. Remember, this is the planet of change. So I would like to suggest you let the creating go on as it will, and be the observer of all the creation. Get your awareness off wanting things to be different. Just remember, anything you create outside yourself in the hope it will give you lasting happiness, peace or contentment, *will fail to do so.*

Strength is power and strength leads to awareness. Feeling strength carries you toward pure, conscious awareness. Feeling your own strength over and over again contains the power to reveal pure, conscious awareness. Strength itself does not rise and fall. Your sense of, "Now I am strong and now I am weak," comes and goes and has to do with your sense of how strong your ego is at the moment. The kind of deep, abiding strength within that is present in the midst of victory or defeat, getting your way or not getting your way, being yelled at or being embraced, *remains the same.*

Any time you feel yourself to be even the slightest bit afraid, I would like to suggest you consider using the following exercise immediately. *Please select, out of all your fears, the one you would rank as the most difficult, the most obvious, the most joy-destroying of all the possibilities. Close your eyes and visualize your fear coming upon you as a reality. See it happening to you. Don't run. Make it as real as you can. Feel the fear, the tightness, the helplessness, the anger. Then, when the feeling of fear is at its height, bring into the situation, whatever it is, your own inner, powerful strength. Nothing changes in the event you have pictured, but now you add the feeling of strength in the midst of the horror and see what happens.*

Pause until finished.

Fear can make you immobile, leave you unsure of how to act, how to move. When fear is at work, it clouds your consciousness, keeps the probabilities and possibilities hidden, and submerges you in pain, suffering, and a sense of failure. Strength is an energy that calms everything down so choices can be made from a place where no fear is present. In that calm clarity, new directions are possible. Begin to live from that deeper level. When you call on your own strength, it has a motion, an exuberant, effervescent action to it. And it increases as you use it. It points the finger of awareness back inside to who you are and what you are, instead of out there, where no real knowing is possible.

My friends, I am trying to impress upon you the knowledge that you have vast energy fields of strength available because they are not your own. Knowing they come from the Source will make you stronger and more secure. Then one day you will be fearless. But until you are fearless, you will be unhappy. Fearlessness comes from an intimate relationship with strength. It is the ability, in the moment when something appears terrifying, to really know all is well, to know you are so filled with the strength of the Source that whatever is happening is alright.

An Exercise In Deepening
April 16, 1989

Any skill becomes yours through practice. The skill being developed here, is how to move past the surface of life and into its center, the center of Being.

Select a partner. Decide who is person A and who is person B. In increments of half a minute, person A, with their eyes open or closed, begins to talk about themselves. It doesn't matter what is said, just start anywhere in your life with whatever feels appropriate. While you are doing the speaking, you may feel self-conscious, you may have difficulty talking about yourself to someone you don't know or someone who may or may not care about what you are saying. But just stay with the feeling of embarrassment, don't analyze it, explain it, or try to get away from it. Simply feel it and continue being aware of all that is going on as you talk. When 30 seconds are up, switch positions. Now you are person B. With eyes open or shut, person B listens carefully, freely, openly. You 'feel' the words you are hearing, 'touch' the sounds with your ears, and allow the sounds to enter you without judgment or thought. Continue shifting from person A to person B until you feel complete in each position.

Pause until completed.

Now, take your pencil and paper and answer the following questions. First, which was easier for you, A or B, and why? Second, what was the main focus of your conversation, past, present, future? Pain, joy, health, love? Third, did you feel more embarrassment at the start of the exercise or later on? And fourth, did you get any feeling, not a thought but a feeling, about your partner? About yourself?

End of exercise.

There will be many responses, all of them 'right.' For example, was there some point at which you felt there was just one dialogue going on, where one psyche stimulated and nourished the other, and then they blended into One? Is it possible to say, even in that short period of time, that some degree of trust and caring was established between you?

Remember the true statement 'Be Still and Know'? When words have died and ideas are put to rest, Truth can surface in your awareness. But people are afraid of silence. What was your response to it? Was there a feeling of embarrassment? Did you feel an impulse to fill the silence? Some people take on the job of filling the silences of the world and others simply wait to hear what others have filled the silence with and then respond. Which one are you? Can you simply allow silence to be present, trusting that in the silence truth can come forward? In this exercise you will 'learn' more about your partner in the feeling tone of silence than in any understanding of words spoken. Remember the basic truth, you are all connected, not through the physical, but through the deep reaches of the One Mind, that which you call the God-Self. And the God-Self is best felt in silence.

I am asking you all to be teachers and learners of silence. You can teach and learn that silence is not fearful and empty, but deep, meaningful and abundant. By sharing silence with others, you will find yourself trusting and embracing them in a new way. Just remain present with heart open, eyes alive, willing to share and care and be silent. It is an exciting moment when you deeply realize that silence is not nothing, but something—something very alive, safe and deep. You come to your simplicity through silence. The ego enjoys complicating things and small mind quickly enters the game with the result that you are confused, off balance, and unsure of action. But in silent listening, you find the simplicity of the feeling of what is present and who is present. This puts you past the realm of ideas of who you are and who they are and places you in the knowing of the similarities that you all share. That which you feel a similarity with, you trust. Things which seem unlike you make you fearful. Your egos are very different in their past, present and hopes of future, so egos fear each other. But in the silence, with the recognition of similarity, fear quiets down, leaving the area of the heart open to love and joining and acceptance. Silence leads you from the unreal to the real, past appearances and into the Truth of the One who is the All.

Safety

Did you ever wonder how you keep as safe as you do as you move about this busy planet of yours? For example, millions of you cram yourselves into moving cars, hurl yourselves down very small ribbons of asphalt, going in all directions, surrounded by lights, noise, animosity, heat, rain and snow, and you are still here. Why? Because you are far more than you know yourself to be. I keep trying to awaken in your memory that you are not limited by your physical body, and that your physical vehicle is the least important of all the vast energy fields that are available to you. Your energy runs far out in front of you, making roadways, assessing situations, feeding information back to the physical computer you call the body. Your energy field also extends backward, behind you, leaving trace fragments of what you experienced in that moment you now call the past. This becomes important when you decide that you wish to move with greater assurance and power in your daily life. Future events have impact upon your physical body in the present. Past events have information usable in the present. The job is to relax in the moment, allowing your limited ideas to quietly subside, to imagine your energy fields as extending deeply into the future and back into the past, deeply into the God-Self within, and to the Light, which permeates all consciousness. Seated quietly in the moment, relaxing into expansion and allowing the energy fields to enlighten you, you will find decision making far easier and more delightful than you are now experiencing. Inspiration about future action will be present. You have 'at your fingertips' data banks past your wildest mental imaginings. As the willing receiver of these strands of wisdom, assurance and direction, you will find you have much more courage to attempt the unknown. You will feel a sensation of rightness because you are doing that which is as close to 'right action' as you are capable of.

None of you need ever be bored. The feeling of boredom is present as a cover, keeping you from feeling 'what is,' now. Boredom, simply stated, is a lack of allowing feeling to take place. You fear feeling because you imagine that your dark side will be what you will feel, but may I remind you, the way through to the Light is to simply allow the dark to be present, not judging it, not hiding from it, and most of all, not explaining it. Feelings of darkness and guilt are present until the Light caresses those feelings and turns the cold darkness into the warmth of the Light of Love. Simply sit, acknowledging the feeling of the presence of darkness and pray from your heart for the Light to show you the Truth of who you really are. You are not the dark. You are in a dream that tells you that you are capable of being dark, but it is a dream, and as in all dreams, it is possible to awaken. You awaken by asking for the Light of Truth to come forward from the Source of your Being and flood the false pictures you have of yourself with its Light. You, as you are now, with no need to change anything, are the way to the Truth and the Light.

Different parts of your body give you different information. All of you are seeking information: what best to do, how best to do it, what kinds of things are most and least appropriate, how to make life choices. Most of you will find you go to your mind for answers and it is true your mind can give you a certain kind of information. *Do a quick test here for yourselves. Present yourselves with some problem, quiet down as best you can, and concentrate first in your mind, writing down what images, thoughts or suggestions come. If you don't have a problem, allow yourself to find out what kind of information the mind gives you. When you have finished, go to the heart. Present it with the same problem. What kind of information does the energy in the heart give you? You will find it is not the same.*

You have all the data. You were not sent on this journey without a tremendous amount of insight and wisdom of what to expect and possible choices to make. The difficulty is, you have been trained to go to the mind for solutions when at times there are other parts that could serve you better. What will help you discover this is the quiet, systematic asking, the honoring of the answer, and the clear intention to use the information in whatever way seems best. If you begin with the small things, when the large difficulties come, this 'hidden' body of help will be more easily accessible. You will have a sense of motion because inspiration and ideas are moving in your awareness. You feel ignited with inner power which stimulates your energy field. Things begin to happen.

My friends, it is time to close, and from the deepest part of me, may I say to you that you do not achieve that peace, that joy, that knowing of Light you are looking for, unless you have the dedication "to love the Lord thy God, with all thy heart and with all thy mind." Please take a few moments to ask yourself this question: "How, in my life, exactly as it is now, without removing or adding, exchanging or denying anything, can I love the Lord with all my heart and with all my mind every day?" If you seek the answer, using your own inner wisdom, images will begin to come to you of ways in which you can begin to make this happen. The Lord, God, is an alive, pulsating Power longing to merge with you consciously every moment. It longs to fill your mind and light up your heart. So find ways to bring about this merging. There is no feeling, however ecstatic, that can compare with loving God with all your heart and all your mind. It is an experience beyond any description, and is worth everything.

If you really are a son or daughter of God, it is time for you to claim the fullness of what that means. The Divine does not want the worst for you or even the mediocre. It wants the best.

TO LIVE
THE ORDINARY LIFE

May 7, 1989
Sebastopol, California

In our work together today, I hope you will come to understand exactly what I mean when I say your life would be less difficult and more peace-filled if you could allow yourself to be *ordinary*. Your major struggles occur because you want to be the best, the most loved, the most sought after, the most knowledgeable, and these desires constantly gnaw at you. They take you away from your true nature and lead you into forgetfulness. Because of this forgetfulness, you do not remember how totally ordinary you are, and how wonderful that is! You are ordinary because *love is absolutely ordinary*. It is ordinary because it is what you are and what everyone is! It is what everything is! To love is not the exception. It is the easiest thing to do because it is your very nature. Remove the belief you are something other than love, and you will see and hear and feel the presence of your basic nature.

So, let us see if in this first meditation we can touch on this ordinary nature of yours. Begin by paying attention to what your mind is doing right now. Take a few moments to really see what you are spending your time creating. Make no mistake, your endless thoughts do create. As you watch these next few moments, you will see that your awareness floats on the surface of a wave of ego thoughts. You see emotions go up and down, thoughts rise and fall, your life as good or bad, light or dark, endlessly shifting and changing. This is the nature of the wave of ego-polarity. Many of you identify your whole being with that motion. Well, my friends, it is certainly not all of who you are and it is a very bad exchange to pay attention to only that motion.

*Let's move deeper so you have access to a vaster wave than the wave of polarity. A wave that is, in your words, **a Light wave**. Alive within the energy field of every single one of you is a light so abundant, so overwhelmingly alive, that to touch upon it would fill your longing heart. Remember, you are pure, conscious awareness. Wanting to experience that consciousness, focus your awareness within yourself and expect to feel that light. Create the image of a wave of light. If you can focus better on a stationary wave, please do it. On the other hand, if you want to have it rise and fall with your breath, please try that. Or, if you want to just feel the wavelike rising and falling of light moving through you, focus in that way. But whatever you do, I am asking you to be aware that you are pure, conscious awareness focusing on light. To glimpse it even for a few moments changes everything. So, let's begin.*

Pause until completed.

You have the ability to focus on anything you choose—any*thing* or no*thing*. But you do choose some focus each moment. If you want the light, turn your pure, conscious awareness back inside, to where light is. Instead of trying to focus on what's out there, which is ever-changing, find the place inside where you are absolutely safe, where there is no pull from the motion of the tides of the manifest ego.

What you concentrate on becomes your reality. Without this constant turning in, you are going to get caught again and again by the ever-changing rise and fall of the world outside. You are going to continue to believe you are what you see, which is a body subject to pain, suffering, decay and death. But none of it is true. Body is there, but you are *not* the body. You are the Light of awareness within the body. Begin to explore whether this is true or not.

Where Do You Go To Feel Safe?

You now believe your safety lies in paying attention to everything 'out there,' so that is where your attention goes. But is this true? Do you feel safe each moment of your day and night? Let us challenge that belief. Has it worked, this total attention to the outer? Or have things you cherished been taken from you? Have you suffered grief and humiliation? Even in the face of your own experience you continue to believe, "If I just pay enough attention out there, some day I will get it all right and nothing will hurt me." Be realistic. That is not going to happen. No matter how content you might be today, you know at any moment everything can change, and pain can move into your life. There is no safety outside yourself—not now, not ever!

The safety you are seeking is inside. That which you concentrate on manifests in your life. If you wish to have the strength, the peace, the love or the clarity that surpasses human understanding, you are going to have to make room in your day to find it. Some of you say you don't want to have to do anything to manifest those attributes. Well then, don't do anything, but don't complain when you are unhappy, despairing and afraid. The moments you spend going inside and reaching toward your desired state of consciousness are what matters. The truth is, my friends, none of this is going to work unless you find ongoing moments to go within and find the strength, see the light, or feel the love. Even in the midst of being out in the world, when you turn your awareness inward over and over, the inner life begins to reveal itself.

You do not need a teacher to show you this. You do not need an avatar or a saint, all you need is your own pure, conscious awareness. The more simple your approach to this state, the more directly you will experience it. There is nothing else in your day I can see which is more important than turning your awareness inward to find out who you are. You are the way, the truth, and the Light. You are not the guilt-ridden, separated manifestation of earth plane consciousness that your mind and ego would have you believe.

When I use the word ordinary, I do not mean mediocre. There is a vast difference. They are not the same at all. Mediocre is mundane, boring. In a sense, mediocre means you haven't placed the power of your awareness on anything specific with any kind of intensity, so it does not manifest as something dynamic, alive, creative and full of beauty. No one wants mediocrity for themselves, for their own awareness, or for their life.

'Ordinary' is quite different. Please think of ordinary as *simple* as in *uncomplicated*. How do you use this new definition of ordinary? Let us say you are having a discussion with someone who is important to you, someone who is a powerful figure in your life. You are trying to come out of the discussion as a 'winner,' not a 'loser.' Now, if you are paying close attention, you will see that you've had this feeling again and again, this desire for a certain outcome. Your thoughts and feelings are going down the same old road. All of a sudden you ask yourself, "How can I be ordinary in this moment?" The desire expressed in that simple question will lead you to experience a 'letting go' of the incredible drive to be right, to be one up, to be admired or approved of.

When you attempt to be something other than yourself you kill the feeling of the moment. If you are trying in any way to act loving, to be right, to feel better, to convince others, whatever it might be, just 'let go' and be yourself in the moment. It is enough to be yourself, because who you are is all the things we've talked about for so long: light, joy, harmlessness, love, peace, acceptance, whatever you envision the highest to be, and beyond.

Ordinary is the answer. To be 'simple' in the moment will give you a sense of how you can just let go. In the letting go, your bound-up energy is released. The energy that is left can be used in a more creative way. Many of you want to have a good, clear space around you so other people can be there without feeling manipulated or maneuvered. By allowing yourself to experience the incredible wonder of the ordinary, you will create a space that allows other people to also be who they are.

Can you see the difference between mediocre and ordinary? Jesus was totally *ordinary*. In the depths of His Being, He knew He was no different than others and others no different than He. This is why Christ calls Himself your brother. This is why He points out in *A Course in Miracles*[1] that awe and reverence are due just to the 'Father,' the God-Self, and that He, Jesus, is your brother. What is appropriate for the Christ-Consciousness is an ordinary brotherhood. Why do you think I insist on referring to 'myself' as brother? It is to remind you there is no hierarchy in consciousness. None. Brotherhood is what is going on here. Understanding that, you understand being 'ordinary.'

There is only One. If you feel yourself to be extra-ordinary, you are trying to place yourself above the stream of the ordinary wonder of consciousness. Anyone who has expanded past the separated knows there is no such thing as separation, no such thing as 'me.' So you see, when you get into the realm of the finder, there is nothing but the ordinary, which is love, the One, the light, the peace. What is extra-ordinary is the ego motion that tries to move itself out of ordinary and become greater than it. It is the *desire* to be extra-ordinary I am asking you to consider releasing from your life.

Try it and see. Let's say this is an important moment. You need this job, or want to have this moment be one of clarity between your child and yourself, or any number of things. Right there, when you relax into what it means to be ordinary, all the creative power of the moment is allowed to move in and *inspire* you. You cannot create anything magnificent without inspiration and this includes magnificent interactions between people. *Inspiration does not come from the ego.* You want to live an inspired life, so every moment of it is alive rather than boring, dead or tenaciously repetitive. Your lives can be incredibly dull when you are trying to make it to the 'top.' My suggestion is to let go of 'the ladder of success' and fall free. In the free-fall, new inspiration can come.

You are looking for inspiration after inspiration after inspiration in your lives. No matter what you are doing, that is what you want.

With inspiration comes creativity, comes the breath of newness rather than the staleness of the old. This is exactly what your destinies are all about, to be inspired by your Vast Self. And you do it by being ordinary. I know it sounds strange, but all I ask is that you attempt it. When you admit to being 'ordinary,' in that moment you are asking for something creative, dynamic and alive to come in and co-participate with you. In your 'letting go' of the feeling of having to do it all, of having to get it right, of having to appear a certain way, creativity has space to move into the moment. That's what living is.

I have said over and over *life is living you*. You have this idea you are living life, but it is just the opposite. There is a power, an energy, a wonder, a mystery, that is living you, and you keep thinking it is the other way around. But you are not in charge of the show, you are not in charge of the action. If you let go, the motion of life will carry you as surely as a wave makes its way to the shore. The desire to be great is what keeps you in fear. This is true of all of you.

Being ordinary will put you right into the mainstream of life. Ordinary is *equal*. Please don't put aside this concept, because the more you understand what it means to be ordinary in the deepest sense, the more energy you will have. The drain on your energy created by your desires is so extensive, in some cases you can never reach that calm place where you can sweetly fall into the knowing of who you are. Begin to look at your life with the attention and the intention of understanding how to make it delightfully ordinary, and the energy you will free can surely guide you toward the best moves in all areas of your life.

What Is Healing?
In your true nature, nothing is wrong, and a real healer

knows this on a very deep level. The true healer brings that truth forward, which reminds the 'unhealed' of that truth, and healing takes place. The healer has the knowing and the strength to see behind the *seeming* imperfection, the *seemingly* disjointed motion of cellular growth. They see the perfection that stands behind all things. They simply bring that perfection forward and impress their knowing on the part that believes in limitation, and healing is the result. The real healer knows that since God is everything and God is absolutely perfect, then perfection is all there is, and the rest, which seems to be imperfect, is illusory.

Let's bring this down to something very practical. I have asked you to go within and find a sense of your own strength. For some of you strength is easier to experience than a feeling of love or light. But strength is the same as Light, is the same as Love, is the same as the Source, is the same as the God within. All are the same. By yourself you cannot overcome the fears your mind and emotions create, but by constantly going back and placing yourself close to that feeling of strength within, you can experience the deeper parts of who you are. Strength is an energy you can ride to awareness. Get in touch with it and you will feel its energy radiating out of the physical body. Set the intention, "Let me feel strength now. Let me feel the Health of my Being now," then drop it. You don't have to know how this is going to work or where to get the health, just know that as you ride the energy, you set the intention and things will begin to happen.

At the same time, do whatever else the ego feels is necessary to become healthy. People come and tell me they are not going to doctors because in the New Age you aren't supposed to believe in doctors. I look at them and see their grandfather was a doctor, their father was a doctor, their brother is a doctor, and their sister is a nurse. So it doesn't matter what the mouth says, the auric field believes in doctors, and if you believe in doctors you will greatly ease the tension around the situation if you will get your body to a doctor and have him tell you what to do. That takes care of one arena of fear.

Do whatever *you* think is going to help, and do not be dissuaded. Do it, not because it is the only thing or the 'right' thing, but because it helps you get all the different parts of your body and your psyche in alignment. Then you can say, "Alright, we have covered all of the places where healing is possible. There is no place to go except to health." Please, pay attention to this. Don't fall into New Age ideas which have nothing to do with the real beliefs you hold about health and your body. There are a few people who really don't believe in doctors, but this country was not created to believe in non-medical healing at the present time. So, do not ignore your own beliefs about healing. Satisfy them and move beyond. Find your strength, set your intention, and transmute your body.

For those of you who want perfect health, perfect illumination, perfect love, perfect peace, perfect joy, perfect anything—something has to shift, because if left to itself the body will keep plodding along at its own frequency. When you place your awareness on the thought that in God all is perfection, you accelerate your energy to such a rate that disease can be moved out of the cells. This is how one gets healed. If you're in the presence of a healer you believe in, and you can deeply agree to let yourself be healed, your frequency increases with theirs and you move out of the condition. Real healing takes place because you simply move out of the condition.

Anyone who has taken on a terminal illness has done so to add to their incentive to really find out who they are. Knowing that death is approaching gives the person many opportunities to find out who they are. Stay with the issue of 'who am I.' Who is in this body? Who is in fear? Who is in pain? Who's really here? When you find out who you are, you may get healed, but it may be of little interest. The knowing of who you are becomes all-important.

Your illness does not have to depend on anything outside

your body to cure it. Healing is an inside job that has to do with raising the physical frequency. People think when they get ill their frequency goes down. That is not true. The frequency actually goes up because you stop paying attention to the outside world. When you are ill you are not so busy manipulating your outside environment, so you have the opportunity to get into the Self, if you so desire. In the end, my friends, the body is a very wise teacher. It allows us to use it to feel dis-ease so strongly that we yearn for Ease.

Stop now for just a few moments and bring to mind one attribute of Being (peace, joy, fearlessness, light, love, wholeness) you would like to have consciously alive in you as soon as possible.

Short pause.

There is no reason why any of you cannot manifest that attribute by the time you choose to leave this earth plane. The only thing standing between that awareness and you is the fact *you don't want it badly enough*. And the way to want it badly enough is to begin to imagine how you would feel and what your life would be like if the attribute you picked was consciously alive in you. This process is not new. You follow it in everything else. If you decide what you want is a twenty-five thousand dollar car, you do not run right out and buy it. You first convince yourself it is what you need. And you do this in many ways. You think about it, you read about it, you imagine it, you hope it will happen, you talk about it, you work on it. Well, just as in manifesting anything in the material world, you manifest in the inner world. What you want you begin to mull over and dwell upon. You begin to act 'as if.' You imagine your life boldly filled with it and that whole process is what brings it about.

God is not an idea. It is an overwhelmingly magnificent sense of consciousness. It is a total coming to rest in the knowing, past thinking, that all is well, has always been well, can never be other than well. There is a part in you that is wholly at peace, alive and aware. Find that place within you and freedom is there. Find that place within you, and total peace and total safety are there. Seek it and you will find it. Seek it again and again and yet again. That is why you came here. That is what this journey is all about.

---

[1] A Course in Miracles, *Foundation for Inner Peace, Tiburon, California, 1975.*

Your *delight* in the movement of the earth plane is when you dance together. The *pain* of it is when you bruise each other. But don't worry, it's nothing very long-lasting. Take two aspirins and call God in the morning.

THE INNER LANDSCAPE

January 9, 1988
Taos, New Mexico

Your lives often seem to be without choice or direction because you have consistently cut yourselves off from what I call the 'inner landscape.' You are all very used to looking outside yourselves and know the outer landscape well. You know the dangers, the places you most enjoy, and what is interesting or boring to you. But when it comes to the inner landscape, the inner life, *the unseen world,* you do not have the same assurance and familiarity. You do not have a sense of knowing where to go to make deep inner choices or how to work with the intuitive knowledge that is always present within. The balanced spiritual warrior learns to move through both the inner and outer worlds. The *totality* of that kind of journey is exciting, interesting and can provide clarity for your life. And that is the point of this day—clarity.

Through the centuries, organized religion had been denying you access to your own understanding, and even more, denying you knowledge of the God-Power which is constantly moving toward the surface of your consciousness. Instead, you are asked to substitute the wisdom of other human beings to help you decide who you are, and what you should do to translate God's reality for you. The difficulty is, others cannot know more than you about your own journey or what paths you should follow on that journey. So, the question now is: How do you live a life using the help and guidance found in your own inner landscape while maximizing its wisdom in your outer journey?

The inner landscape is real. It surrounds and totally permeates your present consciousness, a consciousness that would not look like it does if the inner landscape were not present and alive in it. You begin to experience it by setting the intention to see and feel it. Your world as you see it now exists because the inner landscape is holding it in place, and as you settle down into the present moment, you will begin to feel how *real* the inner life is.

It is difficult to believe the outer and inner landscapes are interwoven because of the human desire to only see things that are pleasing. And when you see something in the outer landscape which is not, you often assume it has nothing to do with you. You project this unpleasant response onto someone or something outside of yourself. You have convinced yourself that what you dislike 'out there' has nothing to do with you. This sets up a pattern of separation between inner and outer. When you see something you want in the outer landscape, you often assume it is separate from you, thus perhaps unobtainable, leaving you with a deep feeling of incompleteness, of not having all you need. But with practice, you can learn to see your inner landscape clearly and with the knowledge found there, remember that the interplay between the two worlds is continuous and both can be experienced. You come to realize it is this conscious co-mingling that is the job of the human psyche.

There are various aspects of the inner that are helpful to consider as you begin. But first, you must learn how to become quiet, because the inner landscape disappears from your vision very quickly when too much mental activity is present. It takes skill to learn how to have the world of the inner manifest with clarity in the outer from moment to moment. In order to maximize that possibility, you must acknowledge that the constant unconscious outpouring from your mind and mouth is one of the greatest deterrents to that vision. Many of you think *speaking* will somehow join you with deep, clear truth. But you are joined to truth through stillness.

So, what are these helpful approaches to 'inner' and 'outer'? One is called therapy. A way to describe therapy is to say *it releases the tension around your imbalances.* Introspection through therapy gives you a chance to see those places that are out of balance and decide whether they are relevant for you today, or are no longer threatening and can be put aside. With the help of a good therapist, many fears and guilts can be examined and released. This leaves you ready to approach the inner landscape with a more relaxed feeling.

Two other approaches to the unseen world are through the awareness of dreams and the dynamic use of active imagination. You have many tools available. *The difficulty is in learning to look inside as often and with as much belief in the reality of your inner world as you have for your outer world.* This takes practice. It is as if you create an entirely new, delightfully free, abundant, beautiful world and you live in it simultaneously as you live in the outer one. You do not have to die in order to see this inner life, but it is true you must 'die' to some of the habits you have created that keep you always looking outward.

Who's There?

Let us begin our exploration of the inner landscape by quieting ourselves down. Inhale and release three or four deep breaths, letting go and settling into your space and then watching the rising and falling of your breath.

Short pause.

*For this first exercise we want nothing more than to find out who or what shows up. Do not program an appearance. Simply allow the inner landscape to present whatever and whoever it will. Watch the images as they rise and fall. Watch thoughts, watch responses. Just watch. Let it all flow past, aware of yourself as **observer**. When that* *has finished, make a list of what you observed. It can be any number of things—people, animals, scenes, events or responses to any of these. If it is a memory, an anticipation of a future delight, a hope, a prayer, a fear, whatever it is, describe it in words as soon as possible. Writing helps to hold the landscape steady so that it does not move out of your awareness without being seen. Please, do not leave **anything** out, no matter how strange and unimportant it may seem. It is all of your thoughts I ask you to bring forward. The gods and goddesses are there, as are the 'ordinary' things, the pain and the beauty. Let it all flow out with you as observer. So, please practice writing everything down.*

Pause until finished.

What To Do When Stuck

The inner landscape will not be available if there are people or events that have deeply captivated your awareness. As you pay

attention to these captivating interests or worries, whether past or present, the energy surrounding them vibrates so much faster than the rest of your world that you see only them, and the deep peace of the inner world eludes you. You may believe half the fun of your love affair is that it's volatile, or perhaps you unconsciously enjoy worrying about the problems in your life. You may still be caught in emotional entanglements or with someone who has mistreated you in the past. Those types of things keep you stuck, and you do not see the rest of life flowing. When you get serious about God-Consciousness, you are asked to simplify your relationships, not because there is anything wrong with having them, but because volatile relationships or responses tend to keep the waves of your life in such motion that no peace or clarity is available.

So, find a way to gently soften your response to situations in your life. Be willing to let go of the tight control you desire to have over events and people in your life. Let things be as they are. Relax. Once you have quieted down, you will find it helpful to acknowledge *what it is* that starts your landscape moving again.

When you feel movement beginning, pull your awareness into
the present, feel the agitation, breathe and let go of that agitation
moment after moment. You are always looking for something,
agitated because you think you don't have what you need. Do not
worry that you are letting go of your great love affair or your
successful position in life. You do not get those things by riveting
your conscious mind on them. Events come into your lives from
so many places you do not yet have any idea of how you create
your moments. So keep watching your mind and drop into
stillness when thoughts are causing agitation. Watch and be still.
It will work if you choose stillness again and yet again.

The Separated View

Everyone has a drama. And dramas in life can seem unending, filled with pain, suffering and personal losses. But your soul
is looking for an opening for you to view your drama without
desire to change it and to begin to see a 'Beloved' in everything.
The Beloved is God—the Light—the One. Fear of loss can hold
terror. But using this fear of loss to understand that the 'Beloved'
is in every place, in every thing, and in every moment, is to make
fear a useful, creative friend. Then you can welcome *any* drama,
and use it to deepen the movement down into your inner landscape where peace and awareness lie. So the release from the
bondage of fear begins by paying attention. Be aware—don't be
asleep. When you feel agitated, this is the time to start your
breathing and let it go. In letting go, moment after moment, the
outer world settles down in a way that allows you to experience
the peace of the inner world.

When you look at the world with just your senses, you see
things as separated. But you don't have to be caught up in and
moved by all the terror that comes from that separated view. For
example, many of you are afraid of death. You know you are going
to die and you are afraid. You are afraid only because you do not
remember what it was like to die—yet you have died over and over

again, and lived to tell of it. Familiarity with the inner landscape can be of great help here, because it contains the memory of your successful passage through death. Because the memory of all your past is found within, the information stored in your inner landscape can remind you death is nothing to fear. When you settle down in the inner world, you can again feel the safety of death, the safety of unseen Life. By going within you can learn to be centered and clear in the midst of *whatever* is happening and it will be a tremendous help.

Let us suggest a way to move through your day: Against all that your separated senses tell you, try to see through the unity of the inner eye. It sees the One—the Light—the Wholeness. So, as you walk, as you move, remember you can see with this inner eye. You do it by reminding yourself that one thing is not more important than another. You look at everything with the intention of seeing the One in all things. You carry with you the intention to see the Wholeness of Consciousness. You asked to see the One Light in the many. Concentrate on that over and over again and it will bring what you seek—a united vision.

A Balanced Awareness

That which you would call the Source, the wondrous God-Power from which everything springs, including you, is *spherical* in shape. The Source is not a linear experience—It is an explosion. The inner core of *your* being is constantly exploding and giving off energy in all directions, which fills the sphere of who you are. Your conscious awareness is glued to only one part of that sphere, your ego-based awareness, while the rest of you is constantly changing, constantly making adjustments and balancing itself. This is not a conscious thing for most of you, yet it goes on all the time. You are constantly seeking harmony and balance.

When you are balanced you move with grace and beauty through whatever it is you are doing. Being the balanced observer of your life makes your journey along the river of consciousness a

lot smoother. You all move with the tide, but some of you are
bouncing and some of you are flowing. To 'go with the flow' does
not mean you allow everything to take place without any effort to
make changes. It means you have all your awareness, as best you
can, paying attention to what is happening so you can move in
ways that will enable your ride to be smoother. In that way you
will know when turbulence is approaching. Most of you stay
asleep until a storm is imminent. It hits, and you say you had no
idea anything was going to happen. But I tell you, you *could be
aware of it all*. The only surprises are the ones that happen to the
conscious part of you which is not paying attention. If you are
paying attention, being in the moment, you will have ample
information available. There are eddies, not only within your
consciousness, but within the consciousness of the planet, and
even within the universe, which are felt by the whole of your
awareness. There is a universal connectedness, a network that you
are part of and experience through awareness. Every time anything touches one part of that network, you can know it.

Thus, if you live your life with awareness, you will know
what things are coming to you. When you have choices to make,
stop thinking and spend some time quietly connecting with the
rest of who you are. Seated in the middle of the sphere of your
consciousness you will begin to receive those messages that will
bring harmony into even the most disharmonious moments. You,
through such inner quiet, will feel the 'rightness' of what is
happening, the peace of the moment, the harmony in what the
ego may see as disharmonious.

You can face anything in this world with great courage as
long as you know it is appropriate. Where you get confused or
afraid is when you are in the midst of something and aren't sure if
it is best for you or if you've 'done it right.' Often you turn to
other confused people in your life to tell you how you are doing,
and to explain what is happening. They would love to help but
haven't the foggiest notion how to achieve balance in your life

because they haven't run their own lives with balance. Don't look outside to others—look within, to that place where awareness brings the knowing. When you look within with quiet confidence, you will feel what is appropriate, what feels 'right,' and what is maximum. This knowing is the birthright of consciousness. And you are consciousness.

Believe It—You Are Limitless

To finally understand what being co-creator of your life really is produces a feeling of wonder. You find you are not out there alone, doing it all by yourself, nor is God out there doing it all without you. There is a harmony in the coming together of your own 'separate,' delightful, expansive destiny, mingling and alive within the Divine power that is constantly urging you toward greater understanding of who you are. What makes your life so enjoyable is your sense of participation in a co-creative wonder in which you have choices. Co-creation is vision-making.

You are all vision-makers. Every one of you has an inner vision, whether you are conscious of it or not. It breaks through sometimes when you least expect it. You have a deep, unconscious vision of how you would like to move in the world, of how you would like your heart to feel, your mind to think, your voice to speak—you have these visions! But if you see yourself as powerless, isolated and alone, you will not have the courage to bring that kind of vision into consciousness. You will *not* stay in the moment and stay aware of what is going on in that moment. But when you decide to acknowledge you can create your own vast vision and keep asking the co-creative process to help, you will begin to understand there are no limits to what you can create. *If you can imagine it, you can create it.* A part of you believes you are limited. Another part *knows* this is not so.

How do you align with the part of you that knows no limits? Constantly permeating your consciousness is an energy field with a vaster sense of things, that longs to blend with your limited view

to help create something excitingly wondrous for your life. Your
job is to keep asking for that Vaster part of you to bring Light to
what you are thinking, feeling or doing. Ask it to guide you.
When it does, fear is no longer relevant because there is a sense of
knowing that whatever is before you can be instantly experienced
as something appropriate. You don't have to get rid of anything.
You don't have to throw out any part of your life. With whatever is
present, that Power and you, in wonderful co-existing collabora-
tion, have the ability to blend, create and bring to your conscious
mind the knowledge that in your awareness is the knowing that
all is absolutely as it should be. *All* things can be used to bring you
into the moment to allow you to experience who you are. Now, as
you are, you are what you seek. You are of the One. Now!

An Empowered Landscape

*In order to help you become more grounded in the inner landscape,
we are going to do a drawing of your inner landscape. Draw a large
circle on a large piece of paper. You have already made a list of the beliefs
and people that fill your landscape. Study each one carefully. Do you
want to feel peace, the knowledge you are perfectly acceptable to God just
as you are, that love is who you are? Choose the one you wish to have
manifest now. When you have visualized and felt this attribute clearly,
illustrate what you have experienced. It might be a single word that
illustrates it, but beautify and extend that word. Give it color, power
and shape. Or you might just use color and shape without words, with
your sense of what it would feel like if you were manifesting that
attribute. This makes it clear to your inner process that you are serious
about strengthening that aspect of your inner world. Hold the attitude
clearly in your awareness as you illustrate it on the page. If you can **wish**
it, hope for it, dream of it, there is already a part of you moving within
the parameters of your belief system to manifest it. It is already beginning to happen.*

*Pay attention to your breath. Be fully **present** while drawing or
writing, then stop and go back to the breath, then creating again. No*

frenzy, just calm, quiet breathing and then expression, breathing, then expression. Illustrate with the calm certainty that you can manifest those attitudes and feelings that you desire.
Pause until completed.

Again and Yet Again

We made the statement earlier that a goal of life is to have as much calm clarity in it as possible. I told you that you can be kept from that goal by the inner agitation of painful past events, relationships or fears. Unless some kind of resolution has taken place, their very appearance in your mind will cause the inner landscape to become unclear. The constantly moving waves in your energy field come from unfinished business. When people die, or loss is suffered, no matter how resolved the events between you, the very fact that someone or something meaningful has moved out of your life causes anxiety, tension and distortion. In addition, if a relationship is unresolved or incomplete, these kinds of endings can cause conflict and create unfinished business. Absent people and traumatic events are as real and have as much affect on you as those actively in your life, sometimes even more, until resolution has taken place. This next exercise is presented in the hope you will use it to come to a resolution around any unsettling event and that it will give your landscape a serene, compassionate, humorous, calm clarity.

Getting In Touch

Take a seated position and for a few moments just breathe in and breathe out. Hold the intention of getting in touch again with the inner landscape. This time, please see or sense a real landscape of some kind. It can be something very simple—a stretch of beach, a forest, a room, a garden, or more complex like a house, a temple, or a monastery. Whatever it might be, there is in each one of you some kind of a beginning spot, a jumping off place that you feel safe in and that's the place I'd like you to go to now.

Short pause.

Try to see your safe landscape as clearly as possible. Seat yourself on something in your landscape, feel yourself seated upon it, get the sense of what it looks like and feels like when you sit down. As you look around, what kind of vegetation is there? What sounds are present? Smells? Is there wind in the trees? Get a solid view of this place of safety. Make it as real as you can.

Pause.

You are now comfortably seated in a place of safety. Those of you who have real, specific events of loss or fears that you have not dealt with, now is the time to do it. Bring that person or memory of your fear before you and begin a dialogue with it. If you selected a person, whether alive or not, have the discussion as if they are present in front of you. You do this by asking key questions, all aimed at finding out what the situation was like from their side. You know your side, now see and hear about theirs. Ask any questions that will help clarify the situation. If they are what you call dead, then ask how they are doing, how it is for them. Be willing to feel their point-of-view, their present reality. This will, in the case of someone you consider dead, make you fully aware that they are 'alive' somewhere—that they exist in some way that your mind cannot define. This can bring great comfort to an aching heart. In both cases, allow their energy in. Then reverse the process and give your statement about what your perception was. They speak and you speak—equal time, please—back and forth, back and forth.

If a specific fear is an issue, fear of illness, of loss, of poverty, the process is as follows. Let us say it is a fear of loneliness. Take yourself forward in time to a place or situation where you feel yourself to be completely alone, experiencing what you fear. Begin to talk about how it feels inside of you, and allow all of the hidden shadow fears to quietly come up. Let them all come and speak to you. As you allow these to surface, you will begin to feel a dropping away, lifting off, opening up of locked up energy. Just watch them come and let them be.

In both these exercises, do not manipulate the energy between you to try and end up getting a particular event to happen that your ego wants to manifest. For example: If someone has left you, do not use this time to force them back into your life to tell you they are sorry for leaving and will return and stay for eternity. That is manipulating energy. Make no mistake, if you do this, the person will actually receive ripples of it. What you are looking for is a calming of the energy so that reconciliation and resolution can take place. Resolution comes naturally where all hidden feelings from misunderstanding and separation are experienced and released. Do you understand? We do not want to create an event, either to pull someone back from death, or to pull someone back into your life in some kind of intimate way. Just try to drop the 'unfinished dialogue' and set your intention to feel the calmness of your Deep Self. "Ask, and it will be opened unto you."

Pause until finished.

There are other parts of your life that can benefit from working with them in your inner landscape. Let us say that a person is not the issue, but there is an aspect of your awareness that you haven't brought to clarity. Say you feel the inability to manifest financial power in the world. This produces a frustration which causes agitation. Allow these feelings to grow strong in you. Push until you really feel them, then ask to have *something* or *someone* appear in your landscape to dialogue with you to help clarify the causes of your frustration. Allow whatever comes to rise up clearly in the space in front of you, and have it take on a 'persona.' Let it be 'real.' Note it carefully. What does it look like? Listen to it, ask it questions. "What do you need? What's gone wrong? What do I need to do to have things change?" And listen carefully, paying as *little* attention to your doubting mind as possible.

Let's go back to the issue of relationship. This time, you want to know why you don't have one, or why the one you do have is not as intimate and deep as you wish. What part of you is sabotaging your desire, fighting what you want? Again, be still and ask for something or someone to arise out of the landscape and personify this part of you. You speak first and set the stage in whatever way feels best for you. "Who are you? What part of me? What do you need to help me get what I want? What is the block?" If you want greater spiritual clarity, ask what the obstacle is and *be ready to hear the answer.*

If someone you have trouble with pops up in any of these dialogues it probably indicates an unresolved issue. We are back to where we began. There is some part of your relationship that has kept things in such a state of agitation that nothing new and inspired can arise. Don't forget, if somebody real comes in, it just means the dialogue is not finished. You don't have to grab them and shake them to make them listen to you. Just be aware that every thought you send down that connecting web of light, the other person will receive. No need to shout, be gentle. Even in your truth, be as gentle as you can.

The Wholeness of the Psyche

The goal of the inner landscape is to have you experience it as an integrated part of the psyche. The goal of your psyche is for you to feel a sense of wholeness, completion, power, rightness, and well-being. The yearnings of unfulfilled desires and unrequited loves are not what the Soul of your Beingness wants for you. When you have a feeling there is a part of you not fulfilled, from the most mundane to the highest total God-Consciousness, use it to move toward wholeness. If you feel your life would be totally alive if you had more money, a love affair, better health, more God, a bigger house, plumbing that works, or anything else not manifest in your life that is available in mankind's consciousness, use this feeling to move you toward a peace-filled wholeness. Go in and address the issue. "Why do I go down the same road to meet the same obstacles? Please, that part of me not in balance, share with me." Almost every time, you find that what you *thought* you wanted is not really very important at all. But first you need to *find out* if it is indeed the cause of your unhappiness, or if it camouflages a greater yearning.

I know that one afternoon of practicing this process is not going to break you into complete enlightenment, but we begin with these steps. You must have faith in the inner landscape, that it has power, that it wishes to aid you and to join with you consciously. Your inner landscape does not wish to be empty, split or separated. So this wholeness within you yearns to share the incredible data it has been accumulating on your behalf, not only in this lifetime but for centuries, and not only from itself but through its ability to go out and accumulate knowledge from all the rest of humankind. This is not the first time anybody has ever been down this path you are walking. You create your reality out of an immense pool of energy, the energy of humankind. That wonderful connectedness of combined wisdom called humankind is a reservoir of awareness you can draw on.

You can train yourself to take advantage of your inner landscape. The rules are simple. You go to your place of safety, ask the situation to personify itself, then be still and wait. When something arises, no matter what it is, acknowledge it and write down what it has to say, what it feels like. Then you respond to it and then again it to you. Soon what you have is a dialogue between those parts of yourself, that for whatever reason, you have cut off. With gentle attention and persistence, that part will be willing to tell you its perception.

There is nothing in your psyche that will stand in the way of your getting anything you *deeply* want. You will begin a dialogue that you may pursue for the rest of the year, or five years, or the rest of your life. Many will begin a dialogue that will bring things into balance and make further dialogue no longer necessary. The journey is to bring you to a sense of wholeness. Little will change if you are not willing to carry out the directives of those parts of yourself that spontaneously speak to you. To the extent to which you are courageous enough to carry out your own directives, that is the extent to which you will find yourself adding to your sense of wholeness moment by moment.

The Choice Is Yours

You have been told there is never any more or any less God anywhere in the Createdness than is present now. If it's all God, there is never going to be any more or less God than is in every single face, event, or experience that comes before you. You must make a choice. What will you see? God, present in All, or separated loneliness? You look out at the pain and suffering in the world and you cannot yet feel that God is everywhere. But by choosing to believe what you cannot yet see, by never wavering, and by asking always to know the Truth of what is before you, the veil will begin to thin.

At birth you come through a thick physical veil within the motherform to get into the world. When you are born again, in the sense of seeing the world with clear eyes, you have to go through another veil. But this time it's not within the mother but within you, and this time *you* choose the birth, *you* push against it. Much of the world says you are crazy, there is no such thing as God-Awareness. But you push against the current that is pulling you the other way, you make your moves, you make your decisions, ever thinning the veil, and then, just as in birth, one moment it's done. Your mother can't push you through this one, but the force that prompts the mother to bring you forth in birth is the force that amasses itself in all its power to bring you this new life. You cannot give birth to your new consciousness alone. When you ask for the co-mingling of your desire to see the Real with God's desire to have you see, great things can happen. Keep asking to see and be aware of what you are doing. *There is no place you can ever go that will have more God than is present here, in this moment, now.* When you know that, you will be born into a new world with a new vision and a new Life. And it's worth everything!

FOURTH DIMENSION AWARENESS

December 18, 1988
Albuquerque, New Mexico

Most of you are striving to understand the wonder-filled consciousness called God-Awareness. And because it is not yet tangible, something you can really experience, you place it far away from yourselves, even outside time-space. So you ask questions as to the relationship of that energy to your planet. Does that energy which you call 'The Divine' ever make itself known on the earth plane? Can it interface with humanity in a direct, immediate, observable way? The answer is yes, it can and it does.

One such event is celebrated by all of you each December with the remembrance of Jesus or Christ. You say, "Let me know He came to earth to help us so we can be like Him." I do not mean 'like Him' in some mundane sense, but to be 'like Him' in the awareness of knowing exactly who you are, exactly who the 'Father' is, and exactly what your connection has always been. You yearn to be able to walk through the experiences of the earth plane as He did, leaving magic and miracles behind you, as He did.

Much of the magic of the Christos' journey is lost because of your tendency not to want to make things seem too miraculous. Christ was a magician in the highest sense. He was able to take all the energies available in any moment, transmute them within

Himself, and present something different to the world. The world did not look like it had looked the moment before. That is a real magician. No incantations, just a very steady awareness, intaking of energy, and letting out something that gives the world a different chance, a different hope, a different vibrational wonder. That is what He came to do and that is what He did.

A gift was bestowed on this planet with the coming of Christ. His sphere of power came hurtling through your time-space and made its way into the energy field of the earth plane. Two things happened. The first, and very important, was that He left an opening which has never closed between what I would call the *fourth dimension* and this one. He made an opening so all of the magic, majesty, wonder, beauty, compassion, delight, knowing and stillness of the fourth dimension is available to you if you choose to experience it. That's one thing, and no small thing.

The second event was that, on entering the earth plane with His new vortex of energy, the Christos was able to accelerate the energy of the earth plane itself, moving it into a faster vibrational frequency. Just by being who He was, He gave everything around Him a chance to change. When His energy started to move toward others, those who were aware of some deep yearning remained in an open state and were able to find the inevitable transmuting power of another dimension. What was available then, in His presence, is still available now in the stillness.

So, what is the fourth dimension all about and how does it differ from other dimensions? The main difference is in 'the one' versus 'the many.' In ordinary awareness, you see duality, opposites. In the fourth dimension you see union. You have a real manifestation of the Christ's words, "If thine eye be single, your Being will be filled with Light." You literally see things without separation. What does that mean? And more specifically, what does it have to do with you?

The 'fourth dimension' is the place where all opposites have ceased to be and all that is seen is seen in the One Light. All is

Light, All is One. It is not the end of seeing, but it is the end of seeing with the separated eye. When you look through your separated eyes, you can see things that frighten you, no matter how much love you have in your heart. Even if your life is perfect this moment, you can look into the future with your mind where all kinds of possible horrors are lying in wait. Projection into the future can cause fear. When fear is present, the consistency of love cannot hold. So what you have is a motion into love, back into fear, back into love, back and forth. Each one of you is subject to this kind of motion because your eyes still see things from a place of duality.

Fourth dimension seeing is not like that. There you would see only what is real. You would see the reality that stands behind the duality you have created. Anyone who sees with single vision is worthy of your attention. An enlightened one sees the drama going on around them but is in no way afraid, repulsed or threatened by what is seen, because he or she penetrates the camouflage of drama to what lies behind. And what lies behind the drama is the One Light.

The Christ was constantly aware of His clarity of vision, and He loved all that He saw. If you could follow His story directly, you would see a man visiting and touching people from all walks of life. His journey was that of a consciousness touching every 'lifestyle' to make sure no one was left out. He very carefully mingled with each segment of the population at that time, joining with them and giving to them of His Being. Everyone was blessed. I want you to be very clear about this. This was not a capricious action. His movement among the people was done out of the deepest knowing that none should be excluded from His grace. None were to be left out.

You may be wondering what this all has to do with you. One of the ways for you to move into fourth dimension awareness is to ask for the help of those, such as the Christ, who have passed through that opening and who stand waiting to help. In every great religion, in every great myth, there is the knowledge there are unseen vortexes of energy, power and love waiting to assist all who ask for that energy to 'come unto them.' They are then lifted through the opening of awareness into the depths of a new state of consciousness. I ask you to use this gift. Christ and others came to make these openings for you, so you can move into that part of yourself you have forgotten.

Many of you who come to blend with 'my' awareness, either through monthly meetings, private sessions, workshops or tours, hold a fear that when 'I' look at you, I might see 'who you really are,' which you have defined in negative and guilt-ridden ways. There is an idea this kind of energy could be some kind of cosmic spy who will catch you out in your dark side. But you see, I *am* a cosmic spy and I *have* caught you out, but not in the way you expect! I can be useful because there is nothing you can do that will frighten, repulse, repel or turn me from you. No matter what seems to be present, an enlightened awareness knows you are only Light. And there is only one response to Light—which is Love. None of the shadow of your personal drama is important. Light meets Light, and that is all. The 'I' of me meets the 'I' of you, and Love is all there is.

We have these public sharings month after month to assure that the openings that have been made stay open for your use. People ask why so many psychics are coming through at this time all over the planet. It is because there are many people ready to move back into the fourth dimension, and more openings are needed. You desire to enter that dimension where the unity of Light and Love are experienced.

In order for us to facilitate that desire, there must be many more 'comings and goings' between this dimension and that one, so the openings need to widen. I want you to grasp this with your imagination, and 'really see it.' The energy flowing back and forth is now becoming much more active. You could say there is much more traffic on the road! Each time one of us comes through the opening, the frequency exchange gets stronger and stronger. In so doing, there is a wonderful opportunity to accelerate your motion upward.

So, in this 'New Age' more are coming in to make the openings available to those of you who want to move outward and upward. Does this mean all the psychics appearing today are 'fourth dimensional'? You will have to answer that for yourself. Do they come with the single eye that has no judgment, sees no duality? Do they know you are all struggling to awaken? Do they help with a compassionate heart? A fourth dimension teacher does not see or care about your lifestyle. They only care about the style of your love, and the focus of your awareness.

So, how do you join with a teacher from this unseen realm? When you see people or countries arguing, fighting and separating, if you could remember what you are seeing is *not really as you see it*, but is in some way a camouflage, you will have taken a step closer to the space where you and the teacher may join. You can only come together in a space where there is no judgment, so do all you can to drop judgment. You do not deny that painful things are happening. They are, but they aren't as real as you believe them to be. Remember, this is the plane of relativity, where things can be relatively real!

The Spirit Of Christ

At Christmas, gifts are given in the name of the Christ. Some people feel there shouldn't be presents and that the celebration of Christmas is too commercial. My friends, given from a loving space, there is nothing more wonderful than giving gifts. Symbolically you are doing this in remembrance of the love Christ represents. They are symbols of the gifts given to you by the unseen God.

But one of the sorrows of Christmas Day comes after the presents are opened and the friends are gone. There is often a feeling of emptiness. It's because the part of you that already exists in the fourth dimension was hoping to break through into your awareness in a direct way. You had a yearning to have Christ Consciousness born in you on that day and it hasn't happened. But take heart. Begin to live from within, asking the Light or the Christ to show Itself, to reveal what is real. Practice, and the magic you are looking for will begin to happen.

You must constantly put out the call. And you must expect it to be answered. You must fall into that centered part of yourself and ask to feel your *own* love, instead of having it mirrored back to you from something outside. You will do it now or you will do it later, but eventually you must do this, because it is your destiny, all of you, to move back through that opening into what we will call the fourth dimension of awareness.

For many of you, your desire for Divine awareness alternates from lifetime to lifetime. In one, you are engaged with all the 'pleasures' of the earth plane. Then when you start to die, you realize you haven't gotten 'It,' and had even forgotten there was an 'It' to get, so you switch to the opposite role in the next lifetime. So it goes, one life of great piety, and in the next you are one of the great 'rowdies' of the planet. Why not? As a good friend says, "It's a hard job being a rowdie, but somebody has to do it."

Finally, that "on and off" process begins to end, and consistency begins to be developed. What has been developing in the last few lifetimes for many of you is a quickening of the yearning for God-Realization. You could say life on the earth plane is losing its sparkle, and you either want to see it differently or leave it and go on to something else. So the yearning part of you has become very active, and the movement toward wanting to know who you are has greatly accelerated. It's a process you are going to experience more and more during the next few decades. But right now, without waiting, you have the *ability* to place your consciousness deeply into fourth dimension awareness while you live out your life on the earth plane. Begin to do it by the simple ways we have discussed or by ways you have discovered on your own.

If you are sincere in your desire to feel the Presence of God, or hear the Voice of God, or see the Light of God, I would like to give you an assignment. Decide whether you want to *feel* God, *hear* God, or *see* God. Be specific. You are all different and you experience energy differently. Choose one, and then, over and over again as many moments of every hour of the day as you can, stop and look for It. Stop and feel for It. Stop and listen for It.

Your physical mechanism is capable of this. If you took a saint's body apart, you would find nothing different from yours. There are no secret switches, no secret buttons, no secret power-packs. You're all the same. Thousands of humans, in their own quiet way, are either seeing, feeling or hearing God in their life now. Not as some vague idea, but seen with the inner eye or felt with the incredible explosion of knowing or heard deeply within their Being. It is what you most want in your life. And since it is, set up your whole day with that intention as the focus. Hour after hour, day after day, after you rise in the morning, before you go to bed at night, every time you have a few moments, remember you want to see, hear, or feel God. I know you think newspapers, magazines and television are interesting, but I would like to remind you that God is far more interesting! And the most wonderful love affair you could possibly have does not feel as exciting as feeling the Presence of God. So if someone you love is not around and you have nothing to do, go for God!

The door is open. Now is the time. If you are ever going to give yourself the push, if you are ever going to take all that you know seriously, I beg you to do it now. This planet is going to make some decisions soon. You are not insensitive, so you must be aware of the accumulation of seemingly chaotic events. As you go about your life, for a thousand moments every day, hold this planet in your awareness. See it glowing with wonder, power, love, peace, harmony and wholeness. See it safe beyond the limitations and chaos the mind of man has created. See all the boundaries dissolving and see nothing but a sphere of energy, unified, beautiful, clear, joined, uplifted. The planet needs your help. 'We' are asking for your help. Just as of yourself you can do nothing, when it comes to this earth plane, without you 'we' can do nothing. Help 'us.' Now is the time.

This is your planet. So please, every day remember it, see it, create those feelings you want for this planet. If enough of you, on a consistent basis, are willing to do this, you will create enough energy to really make a change. But the light, the power and the wonder moving around this planet must move through the beings that inhabit it. And that means you. You are in a position as part of humankind to channel the help needed. Please, do it now.

Many of you have been coming to these sharings for many years. Each time you do, the motion between the 'fourth' and this dimension becomes stronger. As you sit here, you are generating energy and power 'we' can use. So I would like to thank all of you who have attended all these years, because in simply presenting your physical, emotional, mental and astral bodies here each time, you have helped us. Without you, our work would be infinitely harder. So, from 'the All to the All'—from what you now perceive as 'us' to 'you,' thank you. Thank you, and 'we' love 'you.'

Thoughts are the building
blocks of what you experience.
God is the Building Block of
awareness.

JAMAICA[1] WORKSHOP
March 7-12, 1989

One model you have set up in your awareness has been that of seeking many things: happiness, success, the perfect relationship, God. That kind of searching works until you decide you have had enough of seeking and what you want now is to become a finder. When I say *finder,* I mean something very specific. The ultimate finding of Enlightenment, God-Realization or whatever you choose to call it, has a very deep, intense, specific feeling-tone to it. Finding is an experience, it is not a mental process. But you begin by using the faculty of the mind. You start with a resolution to know the feeling-tone of finding. Then you must make one basic assumption. *In this moment, exactly as you are, with nothing added or taken away, you can know you are Divine.*

Ego

Your ego is a creation of your mind and believes itself to be Real. It resists submergence into the Light because it believes to do so will cause it to die. Thus, the ego sets up a series of desires in order to keep you moving from one thing to another to another. It wants you to keep striving, to never be quiet and still. It is essential you understand the only way you will be victorious in merging with the Light is to get your ego to *cooperate.* Otherwise it will fight you all the way—and why not? Why should it choose to die? If you begin this cooperation between you by reminding your ego it will be a part of the wholeness, a part of your Enlightenment, it will begin to relax. With relaxation will come the loss of desire and the peaceful heart of the finder.

So then, how to begin the relaxation. First, you do not fight any motion of the ego. You simply watch it, watch its movement, and see it is not going anywhere you want to go—no place new, no place very interesting. Then gently move your thoughts and your feelings to those things you *do* want to feel and experience. Stop and allow yourself to feel the love, peace or sense of centered God-Presence. The ego will soon learn there is nothing to fear because it, too, will feel the gentle wonder and beauty of the new thoughts and feelings.

The Razor's Edge

Let us talk more about moving from seeker to finder. When you have decided you wish to become the finder, you will discover that your awareness is a great help. But in order to use it you must develop a razor's edge approach to consciousness. You must be willing to watch your thoughts carefully and to realize you have divided them into categories. There is the past, the future, good, bad, judgment, fantasy, guilt, and so on. When you stay with the movement of watching these thoughts, you will observe that you have no real desire to continue being immersed in them. They aren't going anywhere you want to go. This is the point where you call on your awareness to help you keep watch over this process. You gently move your awareness away from these thoughts and place it on what you do want. You do it moment by moment, never trying to push against the tide of thought, but quietly using your awareness to move toward those thoughts, ideas and imaginings that you are looking for.

Most of you are on 'automatic' most of the time and your awareness does not take you to any specific place, but rather is allowed to drift from one thing to another, without any connection and without a definite goal. Finders know that dwelling on the things they wish to manifest in the next moment, such as peace, harmony, love, light, relaxation, will tend to make those very experiences appear. Using the sharp edge of their awareness, they constantly choose to step away from the automatic response into the conscious delight of choosing those feelings, thoughts, and images they truly wish in their lives.

It is important to remember that when you align yourself with the Divine, the simple act of alignment will be a tremendous help in changing your thoughts and actions. If you are feeling Divine feelings, you will find yourself choosing thoughts in harmony with those feelings. The Divine is always present. What you want is always present. When you stay balanced on the razor's edge of awareness, you can have what you want.

Listen

The most immediate, easiest, fastest bridge between you and the Divine is your breath. You, by yourself, cannot breathe. You can talk or not talk, see or not see, smile or not smile, but you cannot breathe or not breathe. Breathing is something that happens spontaneously *to* you. It is the motion of that wonder-filled, extending power called God which moves in and out of you and makes everything happen. So, take a moment now to experience your breath. Feel it rising and falling in your body. This simple technique immediately puts your awareness in your body. Next, begin to listen, no matter where you are. Most of your hearing is selective. You only listen for certain sounds, certain responses. You have trained yourselves to deaden your hearing to painful sounds and in so doing deny yourselves the fullness of life. In order to hear God you have to stop being selective and allow in *all* sound. As you go through your day, be aware of listening. Pay attention to unspecified hearing. Let sound come into you, move through you—*feel* the sound moving through you and watch it with detached awareness. Relax! Do not select. Just allow. And one day, you will hear God.

Seeing

In the end, the pain of the human dilemma comes from a belief that one is alone. You will find what traps you into believing you are alone is your mind. The world around you is asking again and yet again for unification, for the invitation to play into you so that you may *know* you could never be alone. When you do not extend your senses past the limits your mind places on them, you become isolated. Then the senses themselves are the enemy because they increase the belief in separation. When you start practicing extending your senses outward into the physical world, you will begin to relax. You will begin to feel connected with things outside yourself and no longer alone. The physical body itself will participate fully in Being; the mysteriously wonderful experience of being whole, connected to everything.

So let us begin connecting with the visual sense. If you have noticed, the ears and eyes are on relatively the same level. There is a center, located within the cranial structure, that blends seeing and hearing in one wonderful space. Seeing that is done properly is not accomplished only with the eye. Hearing, done properly, is not accomplished only with the ear. If you take an imaginary plumb line and drop it through the top of your head, you will find that center located where the eyes and ears meet. Seeing is a matter of moving your awareness into your head, feeling for that energy center, and then projecting your vision outward.

I would like us now to practice what we have talked about. *Please take your meditation positions. Watch your breath for a few moments, until you feel quiet and centered. Now, with your eyes closed, let your awareness move around in your head until you find a comfortable place where it feels that seeing and hearing meet. Then tilt your head down a bit and look directly at the floor with a soft gaze. When you are gazing softly, your eyes are partly closed and their focus is slightly fuzzy, giving what you are looking at a softness.*

To practice seeing, close your eyes and go to that visual center in your head, then open them and gaze softly at the floor. When you find your awareness on the floor rather than in your head, you know you have lost it. Simply go back to the center within your head, then open your eyes and gaze softly at the floor.

What we are looking for is the sensation of being inside and outside yourself at the same time, joined in a relaxing wholeness. You can do it by staying solidly *in* your skull, moving your vision out and joining with and caressing what you are looking at. The 'seeing' is still centered in your skull but flows outward from there. You will find this joining affects the surfaces of the world in a very definite way. As a result, you and the world begin to feel more and more unified and you begin to feel less and less separated. When you abandon the center of vision inside your head and wander out through your eyes, it's almost like leaving home in order to see things. What you are learning now is to stay at home, which means with the physical, and join with what is outside you.

You spend much of your 'seeing time' out of your body because you are intent on watching what response the outside world is having toward you. You believe you have to 'keep an eye on things' to make sure they go right. This makes you leave your center which results in your feeling even more isolated from yourself. Practice seeing from the visual center within your head until you feel joined in a strong wave of awareness with what you are gazing at. You, the wave and the object become one. When you have accomplished the seeing, add the dimension of listening you have just practiced. Find the vision within, add the sense of hearing from within and see what happens.

Sweet Mystery Of Life
People often ask me why they are here. I tell them they are

here to live life fully, expansively and joyfully. But this does not help many of them. So, perhaps we should not ask *why* you are here, but how you can *maximize* your journey *while* you are here. How can you maximize the earth plane experience, *whatever* your reason for the journey?

If you have decided that life will be meaningful only at the end of it (example: Did I do it right? Will I make it into heaven?), the journey itself is going to be miserable. You will feel you don't know how to live, where your life is going, and your only hope will be that someday, at the end of your life, you will be in the right place and you will be happy. Someday! Please question the wisdom of living your entire life for a happy ending that may or may not occur.

So, how to live? The art of living life is not like the art of playing chess, where only the last move matters. It is an alive process, with each moment as full of potential joy as the next. The point here to remember is, there is a *mystery* buried in each moment, a total mystery. The reason I ask you to pull yourselves out of your thoughts and into your feelings is that your mind, if it could have solved the mystery, would have done it long ago. But it has not and it cannot.

You 'think' you know the answer. What is the answer? "Love is the answer." Someone else says, "No, non-judgmental awareness is the answer." You are both right. But if hearing those words were enough, you would have all, in that instant, said, "Good, let's go home. Let's quit this search." Your *mind* isn't going to solve the problem. The answer to the mystery lies elsewhere. Because you have been taught life is a linear experience, moving from point A to point B, you keep going in linear directions, hoping if you keep on doing what you're doing, you'll find 'Enlightenment.' You have been *doing* this for centuries. You cannot 'think' yourself into Enlightenment. You must *reprogram* your inner message. The old message is, "Keep looking, it's out there." The new message must be, "This moment is it. The mystery is in the moment, just as it is. So, I must be still and find that mystery—now, deeply within me."

The seeking part of you will be delighted to fall into alignment with the new message. *Buried in every moment of breathing, seeing, hearing, is a mystery which, when touched upon, transcends thought and makes you alive in a way you have not felt before.* That is all! Then you go about doing whatever it is you do, but with the total difference of that awareness.

Where Is The Light?

In order to relax into Enlightenment, you have to take the responsibility of relaxing into the mysterious Light and expanding It outward. Relax, expand! Relax, expand! Relaxing deeply within, then expanding the Light as far as you can. It is a *feeling*. Just drop into it. The Light of God is there waiting for you to fall into it, to bathe in it. When you begin to practice this, you allow the bliss or Light of your existence to begin to bubble up and be released. I have told you before, throughout the centuries your cells have gotten the idea they are safest when they hold on. You are holding on to keep your world together. You are afraid if you relax it's all going to fall apart. You have to keep 'you' separate from 'them,' 'this' idea separate from 'that,' 'your' country separate from 'theirs,' while all the time everything is joined. You have taken on an impossible task! At the most basic level, all of you are joined. There is no part of you that is not unified with the Whole. So relax into your bliss, into your light.

Today's assignment is to begin to know the Light is here, now. Please start by making a list in answer to these questions: What would this world look like if you could see the Light? How would you feel if you could feel that Light? Then, all day today, try to do everything 'as if' that Light was present—not only in you, but in everything outside of you. When you forget, try again. Practice seeing only Light, being only Light, speaking only from Light, hearing only with Light and walking only in Light.

Allow Yourself To Feel

Many of you live from the neck up because you fear that anything below that, especially below the navel, will get you into trouble. Various religions preach holiness through forgetting you *have* anything below the navel. But there are times that part of you will demand to be acknowledged. *You* will not be whole until you allow your *whole body* to feel light in it. You *can* be totally Enlightened and in a celibate state, but you do not have to be a celibate in order to be totally Enlightened. Both are possible. It is the willingness to feel the energy which makes both possible.

I am asking you to be willing to get totally inside your body. It is where God lives. God does not live only in your mind. God does not live out there somewhere, God is *here*. The more you enliven every cell of your body with that truth, the sooner your awareness will explode with it and you will be free of the illusion that God is separate from you. Then you will taste freedom.

I am trying to unify your senses so they will all participate. Just as I said your ego does not want to die at Enlightenment, I assure you, your senses do not either. They have done a wonderful job for you. Lifetime after lifetime, they have served you as best they know how, given all the restrictions you have placed on them. They want more than anything to participate in every moment of your exploding wonder, and participate fully in your experiences of all of it! God is not a thought. *God is an experience and you cannot fully feel the presence of God if you are not allowing yourself to feel.*

So, allow your senses to aid you in feeling God's presence. They are not afraid of feeling 'what is' because they do not carry the guilt the mind does. They welcome the Light. They will help you see God, feel God, hear God, and sometimes even *smell* God. Some of you have been blessed with moments when essences of flowers or incense have magically appeared. You have also heard sounds not 'real,' and seen things that just should not be there! Don't worry. Your senses are doing what they love to do—

helping you directly experience God. Your senses are your friends. Use them!

Co-Conspirators

Do you remember this quotation? "Of yourself you can do nothing." I hear the responses now. "Yes, I know what you mean. All the *wonderful, good* things I do, God does with me. Thank you, God." Do you really think He meant He would only help you do *good* things? What He said was, "Of *yourself* you can do *nothing!*" Think about that. Of yourself *you* can do nothing. *In anything and everything you have ever done, you have had a co-conspirator doing it with you called God.*

But you tell me you can't be convinced that God was out there helping people like Hitler. I say to you that you are going to have to make a choice here. Either you are stumbling blindly down a linear path, living in a world filled with chaos, or you and the Divine together are making appropriate life choices that will reunite you with your awareness of God. Please understand that everything you have ever done has been a *co-conspiracy*. And I use that particular word on purpose. If I say co-creation, you immediately move to the light side of things. But if I say co-conspiracy, we are then talking about dark, smoke-filled rooms, where you both sit around plotting dangerous things. Co-conspiracy means that *everything* you have ever done, said or thought has had as part of its energy flow what you call God, the Divine One. Wrestle with this paradox until it gives up its truth. It will if you persist.

Let's talk about guilt. If it is true that you and God have co-conspired in everything, what do you do with your concept of guilt? Now you have a dilemma. Half of the time you blame yourself for your 'negative' actions and the other half you blame someone else. Which is true? Both? Neither? You must grapple deeply with these issues, not in your mind, but with your feelings. *Where is your guilt if God and you created your world and your life together?* Of yourself you can do nothing! Do you really think there are two of you?

I am trying to break you out of your basic, bedrock traditions just for a day. Just for today, ask yourselves if there really are two forces battling for your soul—the dark and the light. If the answer is yes, what do you do with all the people who have come to the reality that there is only One? They've all said it. On reaching Enlightenment they say, "There is but One. I and my Father are One." One! Not, "I and my Father are one and a half," or, "There's a little bit of me and a lot of Him." They say, "I and my Father are One." One what? *One,* period.

When you are being selective you always turn the truth against yourselves in order to hang on to some kind of guilt, some kind of sense that something is wrong. Freedom from illusion comes when you start to live out of quiet, conscious co-conspiracy. If you can drop into the realization that you and your Father are One, and everything you have ever done has been in co-conspiracy with this incredible Power, you will begin to change everything. Start tasting what Freedom from guilt is like. You are afraid to stop feeling guilty. You do not have to *understand* guilt, just learn how to drop it! And you do that by remembering—"Of myself I can do nothing. God is with me."

You are on a journey, moving you know not where. Ramana Maharshi talks about choice. You and your baggage are going from Calcutta to Delhi on a train. You can carry the baggage on your head or you can put it down. Either way, the train will get you and the baggage there, because it is the train that is carrying it, not you. Think about this today. Help participate in cracking these thought forms. Are you the one who gets on the train and carries the luggage on your head? And when you leave the train are you proud of having carried your baggage but find you have a headache?

As the day progresses, watch your feeling-tones. Watch how many times you put the baggage on your head and how many times you put it down. You don't know where all the tracks of this train lead, you only know the destination is total, complete God-Consciousness. How do you know? Because thousands have reached it before you and left that explicit message. So please, put the baggage down. Drop the old and be bold enough to feel in terms of We—you plus Something. If you dare, *it will manifest* and loneliness will be gone. Guilt will be gone. The heavy, burdensome feelings of individual responsibility will be gone and what comes in its place? Joy, light, laughter, letting go, acceptance. What a world you would have! Think about it deeply. What would your world look and feel like without guilt?

There is only one responsibility I ask you to be sincere about. Pay attention to those parts of you that respond to life with power, light, extension and beauty. If you feel fearful and guilty, something is wrong. What you are listening to is not part of that co-creation, that co-conspiracy.

I have thrown out many things for you to chew upon, and I will stop now. Grapple with them. Don't analyze them with your mind, digest them with your feelings. Get in there and munch on them. Find out, are you guilty or are you a part of God?

The Best Friend You Ever Had

My hope today is that you be delighted with the 'stepchild' of your life which you call the body. You have never had a servant as obedient and loyal as your body. No one has served you with as much delight and diligence, yet you treat it like you wish it wasn't yours. You are rarely satisfied with it. You are either too young or too old, too fat or too thin, too tall or too short, always something. The dialogue your body receives from you is never, "Thank you, loveliness, thank you. I am so grateful I can walk and talk and see. Thank you." It's always told what is wrong. The body constantly hears, "Oh dear, look at that, you are not doing it right." The cells get the message *they* are not doing it right. *You* are not doing it right.

Your body tries to please you under some strange and difficult circumstances. It also knows, in the end it can't win because your last command is, "Don't get old." Your bodies know their completion comes in a state of being older. Not sick and crippled and worn out, but old in a positive, dynamic, delightful sense. "This journey is almost over. It feels good, it's working. We are getting where we were destined to go." If you look like twenty when you are fifty, something is truly wrong. And if you have the desire to look that way, you are going against what the body naturally knows. You will constantly be giving it the message that it's 'doing it wrong.' So the cells get tighter and tighter. And in your anxiety to survive in the world, you move more and more to your mind, which you feel can 'do it right.' The mind decides how the body can do it right, not paying any attention to what the body *feels* is right. Your body does not 'think' to create, but your mind does. The mind 'forgets' that the body has its own natural rhythm that can safely guide it.

You Have To Be Present To Practice

You treat other servants everywhere with kindness, warmth and gratitude, yet your most personal servant, the body, receives none of this kindness. If you would change the messages you give the physical, your body would begin to relax. Here we are again, back to the need for relaxation. Relax and allow the process to be what it is.

God is experienced as a feeling tone in the physical body. So, the objective of today's job is twofold. One: If you are not *in* the physical body, aware of what the body is experiencing, you are not going to feel God. Two: The sense of your own wonder, beauty, correctness and perfect place in the world is not felt in your mind. It is a feeling-tone which resounds throughout the body. All the exercises we have shared were given with the aim of allowing you to feel your own magnificent 'rightness' within space. You each occupy a unique place within the Whole and feeling the rightness of that space is what brings delight to your

life. When you feel appropriate in your own space, you can
experience your own wonder, beauty and joy, and it doesn't
matter what anybody else says.

Some people know they have felt the power of the presence
of God. In moments of great stress, anxiety or difficulty, when
you have called for help, a calmness descends and suddenly you
can keep going and do what you need to. The energy around you
begins to vibrate more strongly, so you can feel it and it helps
support and sustain you.

Your body carves a space in the energy-field you call space.
That carved space is alive all around you. As you move through
this day, feel where on your skin you join and move through what
you call emptiness—what I call fullness. To you, emptiness and
space are one; to me space and fullness are one. Begin to feel your
whole body as a form moving through a wondrous substance.
Everything you are looking for is in the space around you. Rec-
ognizing you are safely within your own rightful space relaxes the
being.

To make you conscious of that right now, please take a
moment to pay attention to your feet on the floor. *Stand and put
all your awareness in your feet. Now, rock back and forth, side to side,
then backwards and forwards, very quietly, and begin to feel as you rock
that there is something you are rocking into. One side and then the
other. Don't forget to feel your feet solidly on the ground. That is the
general sense of what we are doing today.*

When you walk, walk as if you were moving through this
substance. Be so conscious that, as you move your hands, you feel
as if you are moving against something wonderful. Feel your very
breath caressing the air around you. I want to make it alive
because it is so alive. This is called practicing the Presence.
Obviously, you have to be in the present to practice the Presence!

Leading With The Heart
What I would like to work with today is another way to

develop feeling secure in the world. We have dealt with seeing, hearing and feeling the relationship between you and Other. Now it is time to talk about feeling with the heart. To feel with the heart is both a happy and sad occupation, until you learn how to deal with it at its highest level.

You have been asked to live your life from the heart. You might feel that's easy for me to say. You could say that since I don't have a body, I can afford to feel life, allowing the heart to reveal all it contains. But what about you, sitting there opening your heart? That can be a very painful experience, especially when you run into closed doors. There are doors within the heart, closed by you in the past when you felt so much pain around some event that you decided not to feel the feelings around that event. When you decide to 'close down,' the unfelt energy has nowhere to go. It just 'sits' there until you decide to acknowledge the feelings within the energy and to release them. Until then, you may respond to these closed places with avoidance, not feeling or seeing the pain. Just like any visitor who feels unwelcome, you will turn and leave. But there has to be a way to open up so it is harmless to you as well as to others. Then you can lead from the heart under all circumstances, in a way that doesn't leave you vulnerable.

So, let us practice. *Please take your meditation positions and begin to feel your breath. Locate it in the chest area, the area of the heart. Make the area wide and full, not a small point that is difficult to find. Breathe into the entire chest area. Feel it rise and fall, fill and empty. For a few moments I want the entire world to be nothing but the rising and falling of breath. Nothing else exists. Let all things flow in and out, just rising and falling. Now, let us try an experiment. As you are paying attention to the rising and falling of breath, let enter into your consciousness either the word, the feeling, or the imagining of the feeling of love. Do not attach it to a person. Just a feeling of love. Keep the rising and falling, and now bring in the feeling of love. Do this until you get a response, however slight. Continue paying attention to the rising and falling as we go on to the next verbal images.*

Pause.

Love is a mystery. What does this mean? It means that anything you think with your mind is a thought, not a mystery. There are no mysteries in words. It is their duty to define. When you turn your awareness to the feeling of love, it isn't necessarily going to be an event or person you remember. It won't be something you've done a hundred times. It is a mystery. *With that in mind, so you won't get an idea you're not doing it right, let's try again. This time, turn your awareness to love and the willingness to feel that love. Allow that mysterious feeling to be released in you. All you have to do is keep focused on it with intention and see what happens. Let's practice.*

Pause.

When we talk about emotional love (parent for child, child for parent, man for woman, or any combination of human relating), the fear is that what comes back will hurt you. Many of you solve this by allowing yourself to risk such pain with only a very select group of people—people you hope are safer to love. But eventually you have to expand past them and learn how to be open and alive to all others. Something deep inside you knows that the goal of love is to be loving—not just with a select few, but with anyone who comes into your life. Nothing less will love allow, and somewhere inside you know it.

I have told you, there is a difference between deep feelings of love that have a universal quality to them and those with an ever-changing feeling of an emotional, personal quality. 'Personal quality' means the quality of relating to a *person*. People differ one from another. Therefore, you treat one person one way, another very differently. Your response to them is based on many things, a few of which include your own emotional nature *and* your *expectation* of that person. What you usually want is some kind of *return* for your effort. If you wish to be truly loving, you must learn to give with no expectations of return. None. The place where you get caught by emotional, personal response is when you 'give to get.'

'Giving to get' equals limited, negotiated love. It means you are willing to strike a deal, to make an agreement. You say, "I will give this energy I feel so abundantly in my heart to you and then I will wait a certain length of time, not too long, and when I feel you return it, I will know we have love between us." A good test for giving to get is to see how long you can wait before leaving if you don't get the expected results. Some people can hang on for days, weeks, some months, even years. Some of you can't last that long. You want it within the day, some within the hour. It depends on who you are and what you are expecting.

The workshops and tours we offer are meant to be pressure cookers to give you a chance to really watch yourself and feel changes as they occur. When you come together with people you
did not choose, it can be a valuable way of finding out what your level of return is. Some of you demand that other people be fascinating. If they are, you will spend time with them and if they are not, you won't. Watch yourselves. Watch your motives for giving. Do you give with one hand and then wait to receive with the other? Do you give only up to a certain point and then pull back because you are afraid of being hurt or made to look foolish? What is your pattern?

Waiting to receive from others is what makes you vulnerable. This places the power of what you are feeling outside yourself. If you get what you are waiting for, you feel full and happy. If you don't, you feel empty and unsure. But if God is everything and everything is One, then deep feelings of universal Love exist and you can experience them without any 'other' having to be present. In all you do, hold the belief that this is true, then look for and wait for that feeling of Love. Letting yourself experience it brings the power back to you. You are in your center of being where the power of Love lies. That kind of *expectant knowing* is what is required. You have thought yourselves into not knowing, you can

certainly think yourselves into knowing. You got yourself into
this dualistic mess by your thought patterns of separation and
you can get yourself out by changing your thought patterns.

I am being very literal about this because waiting for the
return of 'love' is based on the belief that love is something that
can be traded. And you not only trade 'personal' love with others,
you attempt to 'trade' love with God. At this stage, most of you
have a strictly conditional love for God. "I will love you, God, but
I want a return. How long are You going to make me wait? I've
meditated and I've followed the rules. I do everything I should
do, I don't do anything I shouldn't do. Dear Lord, when are You
going to show up?" If God "shows up," you will continue to
adore Him, dwell on Him, long for Him, but if God keeps you
waiting too long, you will leave and seek a more accessible God.
This results in an on and off process of seeking.

A finder knows one thing: *There is never going to be any more
God present than is present now.* A lover who is a finder also knows
this. How do you get to that place? You begin as we did on our
first day. You sing another hymn and chant another mantra within
your being. *Whatever is present is God. Whatever is, is God. God is
present now, in this moment, in this breath, in all I am seeing, in
everything I hear.* You do this instead of saying, "That doesn't feel
good, so it can't be God, it's got to be something else."

Be open. You may not yet believe God is present in everything but tell yourself to try. Wait with expectant hopefulness.
Make the attempt. What have you got to lose? It's that kind of
warrior stance that you need. Everything I have shared with you
these days has been to get you to the point of believing, even for a
few moments, in something you cannot see and you cannot yet
feel. That has always been the dilemma, because the mind tells
you what you are feeling is not God. *As long as you have your own
idea of what God feels like, whatever is present in the moment is not
going to match it.* Ask yourself: "How can everything but what I
am feeling be God?" Either God is so inaccessible you have to go

through lifetime after lifetime in agonized seeking or you stop and jump into the unknown, letting go of the desire for God to prove to you It exists before you commit. Instead, take the improbable stance that God is here now—*hidden in everything*.

You have to be bold. You have to be bold enough to say, "Alright, in spite of the limitations I have presented myself, to my mind, to my senses, I am going to build, moment by moment, the firm understanding that the mystery is here. And I am going to feel it with my heart, my mind, my senses and my emotions. I will channel all of my awareness into staying in the present and reminding myself *It's here!*" Just do it! Yes, it might take a few weeks or a few months, perhaps for some of you, a few years. But with that kind of determination it will happen. And as a by-product, you will begin to feel love more deeply because there won't be any waiting for a return. When you wait for a return, your awareness is divided between inner and outer. God is revealed by placing your awareness within yourself.

Do What Comes Naturally—Breathe

One of the lies you have told yourself is that you don't know how to love. And when you mean the kind of love that egos exchange, you are probably right. That kind of 'love' is very hard to maintain. But the kind of love I'm talking about is not something that you *do*. What I am talking about is something very different. It is a vibrational frequency which has nothing to do with exchange patterns between two ego-based consciousnesses. It is a mystery that is going on within you all the time. And that kind of loving you can 'do' because it is something you allow. You allow it to bubble up from deep within you and feel it overflow into your world. And breath can help.

You have been breathing your entire life. You have not been aware of breathing for most of your life. This does not mean that breathing has not been going on. When you begin to pay attention, breathing becomes manifest, very powerful. You would never say, "I wasn't breathing until I became aware of it. I just started breathing now!" By this same standard, when you begin to breathe consciously and are willing to experience that feeling called love, it will begin to reveal its mystery. And it will not feel like it has in the past. It will not feel like the entrapment that ego-based love has felt like. Love has no thought about giving and receiving. *The feeling of love feels best when it is extending itself.* It simply Is.

So you now sit around and become an extender of love and that is all you are—breathing in and out, being an extender of what is. Real love energy can go to the end of the universe and keep wanting to extend without thought of anything coming back. We are talking about extending throughout all of created-ness. We are talking about a motion that arises out of the Source of all things and has never stopped extending.

Again, how do you do it? You pay attention to the rising and falling of breath in your heart center with the *intention* of feeling love. Visualize it any way you please, as long as it is not connected to another person. In the mystery of it, moment by moment, its truth will reveal itself to you without you having to do anything else. When you find yourself depressed, in a dilemma, or angry, just follow your breath with the expectation of feeling the mystery of the universe.

Some of you are reluctant to do this because you love loving humans and finding love in your heart center seems too abstract, not physical enough. If you think this love is too abstract, not physical enough, you have not truly felt it. When you feel the deep mystery of the universe unfolding moment by moment, you will come to know your body—all bodies—respond fully and deeply to the fullness of love.

And it is impossible to talk about that love without being filled with an amazing sense of gratitude. *So please, a few more moments of practice, with the expectation of feeling it and the gratitude for knowing that it is possible to experience that love in your life. If you find yourself being distracted, just quietly repeat the word 'I,' or Love, or God to yourself until you have moved back into that place of center.*

Do not let the ego fool you. Sitting there and breathing is as natural as anything you have ever done. Do not change this experience into seeking. You have always been breathing, so you can't seek breathing, because breathing is what is happening and it has been going on all your life. That is the model we hold to. Breathing has always been there. *Love* has always been there. How can you *find* what has always been present? Do you understand? This is the razor's edge. The minute you feel there is something to find you become the seeker. Stay with the feeling, and all will be well.

The Back Door

I often remind you that you all have something called a back door. I wish to go into that concept again because I mean something very specific when I say 'back door.' This concept pertains not only to your spiritual quest, but to your life as a whole. One of the things your mythology keeps repeating is the idea of the gods being upset if you are too happy or too fortunate. In some traditions, on the day you are married it is hoped that it will rain so the gods will not be too displeased by your happiness. In other traditions, a beautiful child is purposefully deformed so that the gods will not take much notice of her or become jealous of her beauty.

The idea is that you don't dare to have a sense of your own beauty, worth, power, strength or intelligence. In fact, many of you had parents who punished you for those feelings, calling them pride and arrogance. There is a fear that some payment will be extracted. Somehow you were made to struggle against feeling too good about yourself. May I tell you I have never, in all of my work of the last eleven years on the earth plane, found anyone who thought too well of themselves—ever! Whatever the outer manifestations may look like, the inner feeling is not, "I am better," it is, "I am struggling to convince myself that I am at least equal with others in the world." None of you were raised with the idea of feeling your own energy, your own abundant wonder, beauty, wisdom and extension because of the fear of pride and arrogance which would result in misery. But there should be no blame assigned, for how could your parents possibly give you the gift of that feeling of well-being they do not possess themselves?

But if feeling God is your goal, it doesn't help to believe in this kind of a God—a God who punishes. These beliefs provide you with an excuse not to get on with finding God. 'Back doors' are your way to escape your inevitable encounter with the Divine. A back door is any deeply ingrained negative belief which provides an excuse for not moving to new ways of seeing yourselves, acting with power and 'being' who you really are. It is an excuse you can give to yourself, others or God for not manifesting your Best Self—*now*.

Here is an example of a back door. "The world is a jungle. You have to fight for what you want." Do you see how that belief might stand in the way of getting the peace that you want? Some others, please. "Men always win." "You have to be perfect to find God." "I was born poor and I'll die poor." "All women are dangerous." "Money is the root of all evil." "You are what you are. You can't change."

So, please take up your pencil and write down what you feel your 'back door' to be. What are the beliefs you carry about yourself that keep you in a state of false humility?

Pause.

Someone asked if the back door is the same as the shadow. A wonderful thing about the shadow is that oftentimes what appears to be shadow turns out to be light. Glorious as well as dark things live in your shadow. You hide parts of yourself because *you* feel they are inappropriate either to yourself or to others, and these can be 'beautiful' as well as 'ugly' parts. For example, you may have been trained to believe that the pleasures of the body are ugly only to have it revealed that such pleasures can be beautiful and nurturing to others. The back door is a bit different. When you know your back door, you know where you are paying the price to keep yourself limited. It will always be a view of yourself that makes you incapable of achieving what you want. It is the one thing in your life that keeps you down by telling you that you cannot have what you want because you possess this inescapable flaw. Where do you continue to feel unworthy, and why? These questions will reveal the back door. I call it 'back door' because you all say you wish to have God-Realization, all the time knowing you have a way out, should you choose to take it.

The idea you are less than the Divine is only in your mind. Many of your beliefs rest on the concept of "the squeaking wheel getting the grease." You have to be a squeaky wheel for God to notice you. People will go to any extreme to get attention, because just being sunny, bright, and cheerful doesn't get you the attention or result you want. There is the belief that if you are not crawling on your knees and handicapped with burdens, God will not notice you.

As Below, So Above

Many earthly relationships are based on lack, "Stay with me because I am so incapable of taking care of myself I would be a mess without you." If you have such a relationship here, you may be sure you also have that kind of relationship with God. As below, so above. You cannot say, "I need to keep this human with me because I am such a nitwit, but, on the other hand, I am so bold and wonderful God will want me to enter the Kingdom." Watch what you say because you make these contradictory statements all the time.

You must find the courage to start reprogramming yourself with single-pointedness to be a happy, alive, wondrously abundant, delightful human being. Day after day start acting 'as if' you were, then watch what you do. Do you fall back on your pattern of being interesting through your problems? I'll complain to you, then you complain to me. You save me and I'll save you. If there are only equals, one can't be up and the other down. It's easy not to want to be on the down side, but how many of you want to surrender the up side? That's a deep psychological as well as spiritual question. Taken to the end, you must also see these questions about your relationship with God. If you are busy playing the 'one up,' 'one down' game, you are very likely never to feel yourself good enough to "enter the Kingdom of God."

God Is The Ultimate Happiness

You know, you might be even more interesting and fascinating as an open, happy consciousness, free of problems. Wanting God-Awareness is a desire that runs very deep. If you do not have the consciousness of a winner, of getting what you want in life, when it comes to God-Realization, you will not 'get' that either. You will remain a seeker, because only winners become finders. You must make that shift. Start talking about the newness you want to feel, start watching in your life for all of the wonder, goodness and Light, and let the rest fade. Allow yourself to participate deeper and ever deeper in a mode of self-acceptance. Do anything you need to do to have that happen.

I told you when we began our work together, God is not interested in worms. He wants strong, extending, alive, exuberant consciousness. That doesn't mean you're never unhappy. Allow all your feelings and focus on what you want. The people I find most in alignment with God-Consciousness are robustly happy, positive, dynamic, and caring. They know they are capable of doing all there is to do, good and bad, and have concentrated on dropping guilt and choosing Light, Happiness, and God.

One of the reasons for trips to places such as Jamaica is to get you into that state of exuberance. So, those of you who do not want to be exuberant, don't come with us again, because it will be a terrible strain on you to keep from being happy. All it takes to be happy is to *decide* to be happy. You do not dwell on the 'have not,' but on the 'have,' on the feeling of abundance.

If you keep negating your life and denying who you are by feeling you cannot be happy, or don't deserve to be happy, you will not find God, because *God is the ultimate happiness.* As you get more joy-filled, you begin to feel less critical of yourself. Then you really start to feel good. And feeling good is usually what stops people, because it is very difficult to allow yourself to be happy in such an unhappy world. You are afraid of being happy! But you can change that. You can decide, just for this day, you are going to do your best to look around for happy moments and be aware of happy feelings.

Live out of that desire because you find God through happiness. Have you ever seen an unhappy person who has experienced the God within? Do not sorrowfully wait around for God to tap you on the head to make you happy. That is a vision of the seeker and will take a long time to fulfill. The concept I have asked you to entertain deeply is that now, in this moment, the Divine is present and you are part of that Presence—and feeling it will make you deliriously happy!

There is nothing to find by seeking, nothing to seek, nothing to be good enough for. Stop the idea of separation and be committed to the feeling of wholeness. It takes practice. Do not forget the basic strength of the religious movement comes from telling you the things you have done wrong. Religion is set up to be the negotiator between you and God. But if you and the Father are one, you can do your own negotiating and bring about your own union.

Peace In The Present
I know I am asking you to stretch, but why not? It feels good, doesn't it? It's time to stretch. When you finally get the feeling that all you want to do is breathe and allow whatever seems

appropriate to be said and done moment by moment, you start living in the spontaneous now. So much is conditioned by past and future. If you are speaking from either one you have lost the present. In the spontaneous now, you feel what feels right, and then do it. If you have a difficulty, just express it. Be clear, be spontaneous, be open. Allow whatever is happening to happen without judgment.

To be spontaneously clear and true to your being as it is manifesting each moment, we have to go back to the first day. You must be present in your body, not out there watching faces, wondering what they are thinking. Unconscious dialogue with others is a reflection of an inner, unconscious dialogue with other parts of your being. If you can see it outside of you, you can find it inside of you. You are talking to yourself. So stop talking and begin looking within.

The way to a state of peace is to be aware of what you are feeling. Many of you are not in touch with what you are thinking and feeling because so many moments of your life have been uncomfortable. But then, you are only living half a life. The way to wholeness is to pay attention. What are you feeling? What are you saying? What are you thinking? What's happening with your feet? What's happening with your breath? Stay home, in your body. Pay attention. Be responsible. To feel the flood of life as it is moving through you is enough! That's all you do, moment after moment after moment. That's living life fully, now. Don't worry about doing it 'right.' You are never going to do it 'right.' There will always be somebody to say you're wrong. You will never get 100% approval from the world, so stop trying. When you are at ease with yourself, you will relax. And when you relax, God-Awareness, the Light, begins to move. And when It does, you feel it. Get your own approval. And that is enough.

You Are What You Seek

We began with the plea that you move to the consciousness

of the finder, a state of consciousness where you can find what you need in every moment. You are constantly creating in each moment, and any time you move your awareness out of the present moment, you move away from the creative part of yourself. And you want to be in touch with that creative part because it is the part of you that can help you create what you want. Pay attention to what is going on in and around you and you will deepen your awareness and know exactly who you really are. You are not a linear mind struggling against some kind of chaotic moment in time-space. You are an ever expanding, magnificent explosion of light, sound and color, constantly in motion, fulfilled and filling each moment. There is nothing complicated about any of this, simply be willing to stay in the moment and experience it.

I have enjoyed this week for a particular reason. It is the first time I have had the opportunity to be with all of you on a daily basis for a long period of time. It has been of great help to me and I have learned much. During this week you created more energy than you need, so with your permission, I will take it to places in these islands, on this planet, that have need for what you created.

Most of you I will see again and that will be my pleasure. Those of you who I will not, please remember: *You are what you seek. You are what you want. You are that!* When you remember this moment is all there is and nothing needs to be added or taken away, you will find your life beginning to transform itself.

Perhaps most of all, I ask you to remember something you cannot yet see, that the power of the Light longs more than anything to consciously and creatively share your life. As many moments of the day as you will allow, by inviting it in, the power will be present.

I thank you all for coming this long way. I thank you for your care. I thank you for your laughter and I thank you for your willingness. But most of all, I thank you for your love.

[1] *Inward Bound Tours are composed of groups of people seeking their spiritual awakening, who spend two or three weeks touring parts of the globe that Bartholomew feels have transformative power. Bartholomew is available for one hour each day to maximize these opportunities. The tours are arranged by Friends of Vista Grande, P.O. Box 1656, Taos, New Mexico 87571.*

THE NOW
OR NEVER MOMENT

April 23, 1989
Albuquerque, New Mexico

As many of you know, we are approaching the time of the year in which we celebrate the Enlightenment of the Buddha.[1] His gifts to world consciousness are many, each part containing a sense of the calm and the peaceful and the clear. From the time of His illumination until His death, we see Him moving now here, now there, quietly sharing His Light with ever increasing numbers of God-hungry people. His teachings took place in nature. Quietly surrounded by trees and animals, His was a sharing not so much of words, but of the essence of what He had awakened in Himself and become. And what had He learned upon awakening? That he was pure, conscious awareness, manifesting as that entity you call Buddha. This planet has been deeply altered as a result of His Awakening. He helped the planet in the past, and can help you now, today.

If you knew Buddha Himself had reincarnated and would present Himself for quiet contemplation in this hall every morning at four o'clock, the place would be packed. It wouldn't be able to hold the number of people willing and delighted to come and participate in that calm, quiet energy field that He represents. But when you are told His energy field is still available to you in a very deep, real, decisive, extending way, even if His body is not, doubt arises. If you can't see him, how can you know His wisdom is still available to you? Why not find out for yourself?

It works like this. The coming of the month of May reminds lovers of Buddha of the gratitude they have for His perseverance and victory over the illusion. They set aside one day to share this gratitude, and as they send this combined energy out into the universe, it forms a wave. You can 'ride' this wave by joining your consciousness with those who are participating in this Festival of Light. At such moments, much light can enter your awareness because of the accumulated, focused energy field of love and gratitude that you are now a part of. When these special times of celebration come around, the energies are in such a position that deep understanding and unfoldment are possible. But nothing is going to happen if you are not there to receive it. You would do yourself a tremendous favor by finding time, as many moments as possible, to attune to this alive vibration, to sit quietly in full anticipation of feeling an awakened response. In the end, all of the teachings say the same thing, "Be still and know." That is the deep message of the Buddha.

The Heart And The Mind

Oftentimes, people see Jesus as representing the Love of the Heart and Buddha the Clarity of the Mind. In fact, if you sat in the presence of either of these two magnificent Bringers of Light, you would not feel any difference whatsoever! Both carried the message that something very, very simple is going on right now, within you. And that mysterious, unseen 'something' is felt as both an upwelling of Light in the mind and Love in the heart. Their teachings were simple. In their lifetimes, there was no necessity for an external organization. Where is the temple? The temple is inside you. Where do you go to pray or meditate? It doesn't matter. Just sit down, be still, and know. Move away from the thoughts of the rise and fall of life and allow that which is the gift of God-Awareness to rise up and fill your heart and mind, and know who you are. I bring this up again at the time of the Buddha energy because all of the power and energy of the great Illumined Ones is still present, as a gift of Their Grace. That wisdom is not separate from you, except insofar as you believe it to be.

How did Buddha come to such a state? One day, after going through years of austerities, He decided that something wasn't working. He was down to one grain of rice a day, was sex free, and just sitting around in silence. Then there came a moment when He realized that all the austerities hadn't awakened Him to who He was. In that moment something happened within Him. He came to that place of 'now or never.' He vowed to remain where He was until either He knew His True Nature or death overtook Him. Fortunately, knowing arrived first.

Many of you *have not yet reached that 'now or never' moment.* You are still hoping the next love affair, or the next job or next something is going to bring you happiness. My friends, be careful. When you keep looking for the next ego gratification, you are also saying, "Next lifetime." If you believe the moment to experience God is not now, the cycles will continue.

One tremendous aid to bringing this moment closer is to imagine what your life would be like if you were fully illumined. Most of you never entertain the idea at all! You never sit in your home and say to each other, "How would we act if we were illumined? How would we feel about each other? What would we say? And most of all, what would that feeling be like inside?" You don't talk like that. No blame, but it isn't even a possibility that enters your awareness. You spend most of your time trying to solve the problems that exist in the situations you are in. I am not saying you should not solve problems. I am saying, if you would begin to allow yourself to dare to dream the unspeakable dream of being free of pain, suffering and sorrow, if you would begin to imagine how that would feel, you would begin to get excited about feeling your own freedom from limitation, and that would bring the 'now or never' moment closer.

You have been told to believe that you are limitless. But do you really believe it? Do you really believe there are no boundaries? There may be confusion about this sense of limitlessness. Who or what is limitless? I did not say your ego is limitless, and aren't you glad? I did not say your enemy's ego was limitless, and aren't you very glad? But there is a part of you, your magnificent Christ-Nature, Buddha-Nature, God-Nature, that *is* limitless. And you have the ability to know that limitlessness. But it does not happen without commitment. Until you decide that it is your single-pointed reason for living, you will not be able to amass enough energy to have it open to you. You are not free of the sense of limitation because you are not yet interested enough in its happening. But the time will come when you will be. Do it now or do it later, but you will do it. It is your destiny.

Our part of this journey we are taking together is to encourage you to continue. The goal is real, it can be achieved. We are

trying to entice you. It's as if a brand new planet had been discovered and we want you to come and visit it. The best way to do that would be to tell you where it is, what it feels like to live there, and what is available there. And that's all I'm doing, trying the best I know to entice you to become interested enough in your own freedom so that it is your reason for being.

Many of you have identified completely with your roles of duty and obligation, and your life has become a series of 'have to's' and 'should's' with a 'want to' occasionally thrown in. My friends, that is not what your Creator had in mind when all this started. The idea that you have to hang on to life, struggling through event after event with only some small reward at the end, is not the purpose of life. The idea was to have you arise in the morning, grateful for another day to live in your body, to feel the motion of its power, and to be aware of the joy-filled feelings of Life moving through you. It was to have you feel as much of that amazing, empowered Life as you possibly could, and to extend that wonder into all you do.

Now, how can you help yourself to shift into this way of

Being? Let us say, you go to the office and you have eight hours of paperwork ahead of you. Most of the time you use your hands, because that's what moves the paper, and your minds, because that's where you think about what you are doing. But if you focus only on hands and mind, you are missing the entire point of what your 'paperwork' is for! The point is not to plod through reams of paper every day. From the soul of you, from the eternal part of you, the point of the exercise is to continue doing the paperwork, but with an added focus. And that focus comes from staying in the moment, conscious of all that is going on, all you are doing, but with the added intention of feeling the God-Presence as you do what needs to be done. Put your attention on the observer that is watching the action being performed, and then see what happens. This simple technique takes away much of the struggle or the boredom, and brings in the Power of the Presence. It empowers *any* action you are performing, making even the most difficult or most boring activity a Godsend. It changes everything. Paperwork, done alone, can drive you to distraction. But paperwork done with God can carry you to the Light.

Remember, don't look *outside*. There is nothing you can do outside that is going to create this feeling in you. Remember the possibility of enlightenment. When you dare to entertain the idea of what it would feel like to be enlightened, to be exuberantly alive, moment after moment, you bring that aliveness toward you. Then you move out in the world and whatever is to be done is done from this deep inner place. You live from a place of power. None of this is based on changing anything outside. Buddha and Christ would not bother to ask you to change your job, your relationships, or anything outside yourself. Their only statement would be, "Go within."

The Human Condition

I would like to throw out a challenge. Some of you have lives so safe, so secure, so insulated, that you have forgotten what it is like to be a part of the human condition. But you are a part of the whole, a part of all that is going on. So I would like you to try something. As you look at this globe and all of the things going on upon it, remind yourself that *this* is what it means to be a human. You might not be there in the thick of war or famine now, but you very well might be next time around. Any moment things can start to shift and move for you. Let this exercise help you not to fool yourself as to how safe you are. You could, in a moment, lose something or someone you deeply cherish, or all that you have built up could crumble. Change is happening all around you. Don't wait for painful events to create the desire for enlightenment. Remember you are a part of humanity, and anything that could happen to one of you could happen to all of you. Use this possibility to increase your desire to be free from suffering. Don't wait!

You are a part of the whole. You are not separate from any of the things you hear or read about. Whether you are manifesting them in this moment of this lifetime or not has nothing to do with anything. You are One. If you will look at and understand what this globe is going through, you will begin to feel a kind of nervous anticipation. It is the natural response of anyone who realizes there is only one planet and one human condition. If you begin to be alive to what is really going on in the human drama, you are going to want to become Self-Realized. The pain of mankind is there, so use it to pull you to God. In so doing, you will help the suffering of the world.

You have been told that it is a privilege to be given the opportunity to take a human birth. Why? Because it presents you with the opportunity to discover your Buddha-Nature or your Christ-Consciousness, and to help to eliminate suffering for yourself and others. So do not isolate yourself from that suffering. Be open and alive to it all. Buddha and Christ can help, but the responsibility is yours. Keep remembering that there is an answer to suffering and that it can be found right here, right now.

And as you begin to awaken to the answer, you help all of those who suffer. Your discovery helps them to also discover the truth. It becomes a golden chain of moving power, leaving light where there was darkness. Light awakening Light.

Please, don't ask for an easy life. Ask for the strength to accept whatever life brings, facing whatever happens with power and awareness. An easy life may lull you into the belief that somehow you are separate from the incredible pain and agony and confusion on this planet. Don't hide. Open up. Hear whatever you need to hear. Feel what is there to feel. Now is the time. My friends, don't wait for things to get worse.

When you are having a difficulty, ask yourself how you and the difficulty would look in the light of illumination. How would you work with it, what would the action be, if you knew you were totally Self-Realized, with nothing to fear? Truly, the only gift 'our side of the Light' can give you is to keep reminding you that you have available to you the knowing that you are Light, that you are Peace, that you are Joy, that you are safe.

Many of you say you lack intensity. So, you cannot keep focused on the desire for God-Realization. Whatever you are giving your attention to is what is most attractive to you. If what is most attractive to you is a certain lifestyle, your children doing the right things, or large amounts of money, then you will never fall into the arms of God. You gather God-intensity through practice. So practice. Practice with your imagination all day. Stop what you are thinking and get inside and practice. Practice God! Stop running, just live to know your True Nature. That's all the Buddha would have to say. That's all the Buddha did say. That's all They ever say. And there is going to come a time when that's all you are going to say.

So, again, instead of insulating and isolating, I am asking you to do the very opposite, which is participate in the human fear, in the human condition. Allow yourself to have the humility to know that however your life might look right now, you are a part of that condition. You are no different from any of it. This is one planet, one people, one life, and to the extent you do not know that, you do not know a part of yourself. If you really believe you are not capable of extreme negative action under terror, then you do not know yourself. Open. Don't be afraid to open and know who you are, and whatever you see in this world, that is who you could be, who you have been, and who you may be again. Isolation breeds a sense of superiority, and superiority ends in stupor, in dreaming. Don't sleep. Find out what is here, and in the seeing, you will realize the only way out of this dilemma is to know what is really happening behind all the pain, the war, the suffering and the starvation. Behind it all, something is happening. Find out what!

We end as we began. You are all participating in a dream, a dream full of pain, separation, and death. Remember: Adam fell into a deep sleep, and nowhere does it say he woke up. But awakening from that dream is humankind's destiny. And these words are presented to assist you in that awakening. They carry with them the deep hope that they may be a part of the *wings that fly you Home.*

174

---

[1]The full moon in May, often called the Wesak moon.

The flower of your enlightenment is in bloom. It could never do anything but be in bloom. But if you take a smaller view, say that of a tiny insect making its way up the plant, starting at the base and slowly crawling through and under the leaves, onward and upward, you will not see the flower of enlightenment is already in full bloom.

At one period of your growth, you see yourself as that tiny insect, making its way up the stalk, listening to others encouraging it on. Then comes another stage, when you want to drop the idea of yourself as beetle separate from plant, from flower. You move away from the idea you are a body and remember you are pure, conscious awareness, manifesting as beetle, as stalk, as leaf, as flower, as the space that surrounds it and far vaster, past all your wildest imaginings.

You are limitless, and that knowledge is yours. You are pure, conscious awareness, manifesting in millions upon millions of forms. And when you withdraw your identification from your one small form and simply allow that 'something Vaster' to impress itself upon you, you will know the flower of enlightenment in full bloom, open and fragrant, as it has always been.

People often say they want it all. Don't want it all—*be it all*. You are that which you are seeking. You do not have to traverse *anything* to reach it. But, my friends, the price of admission is your decision to withdraw from the concept of separated self. Simply begin to live each moment for one reason only: to have the knowledge that Enlightenment is present right here, right now, reveal itself to you. I come to remind you the Divine is totally available to you now. It is my prayer that the power of my knowing will join with the power of your knowing so it will also be true for you. There is but One Self, my friends, One Self, and *you are It.* ❧ **Bartholomew**

BOOKS BY BARTHOLOMEW

"I Come As A Brother"
A Remembrance of Illusions
Throughout Bartholomew's simple yet profound teachings, there is a deep sense of love and compassion for all existence. Fourteen transcribed sharings deal with our relationship to ourselves, each other and the Divine. From sexuality to St. Francis, Bartholomew's wisdom and humor point us toward a more expanded consciousness.

From The Heart Of A Gentle Brother
Responding directly to personal questions, and providing powerful spiritual exercises, Bartholomew leads us on a search for peace within and freedom without. Exercises and effective techniques, and also much in the way of wondrous messages that open the eyes of the spirit.

Reflections Of An Elder Brother
Awakening From The Dream
With an unyielding desire for us to open to our true Selves, Bartholomew offers wisdom and guidance yet again, to help us claim our birthright of experiencing our oneness with the Divine. Anyone who is seeking to reawaken that experience will find much comfort in his basic message that we only need awaken to who we are to find that which we seek.

Planetary Brother
Bartholomew continues his communications on wholeness with more spiritual insights that penetrate into the deepest essence of our lives and our beings. In the fourth book of this best-selling series, Bartholomew explores war in the Middle East, co-creating realities, the Divine use of relationships, expanding awareness, and other planetary issues.

Each book $13.95 prepaid, U.P.S. postage included.

HIGH MESA PRESS
P.O. Box 2267
Taos, New Mexico 87571
Phone/Fax 505-758-8769